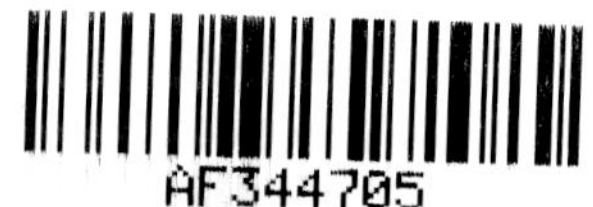

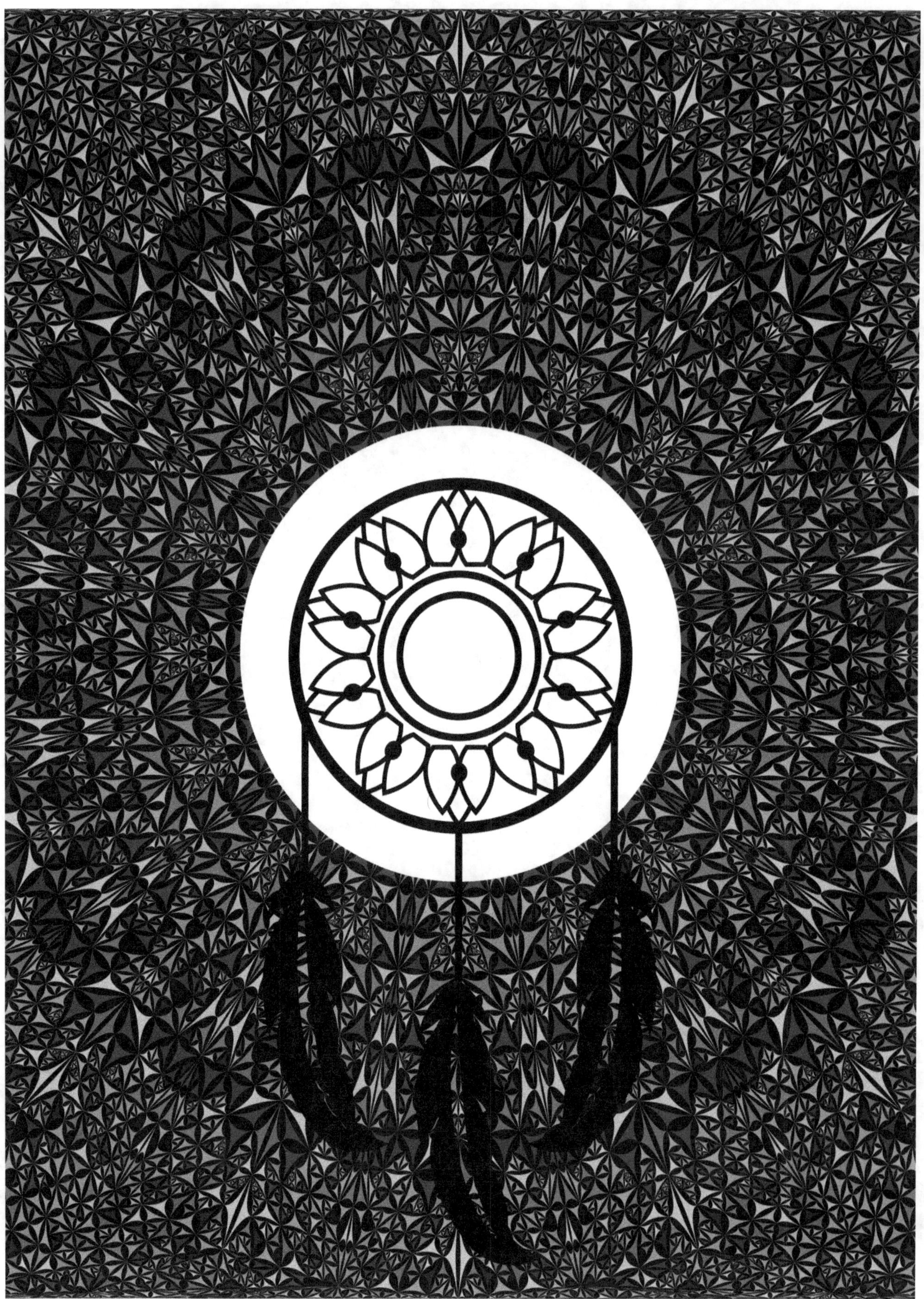

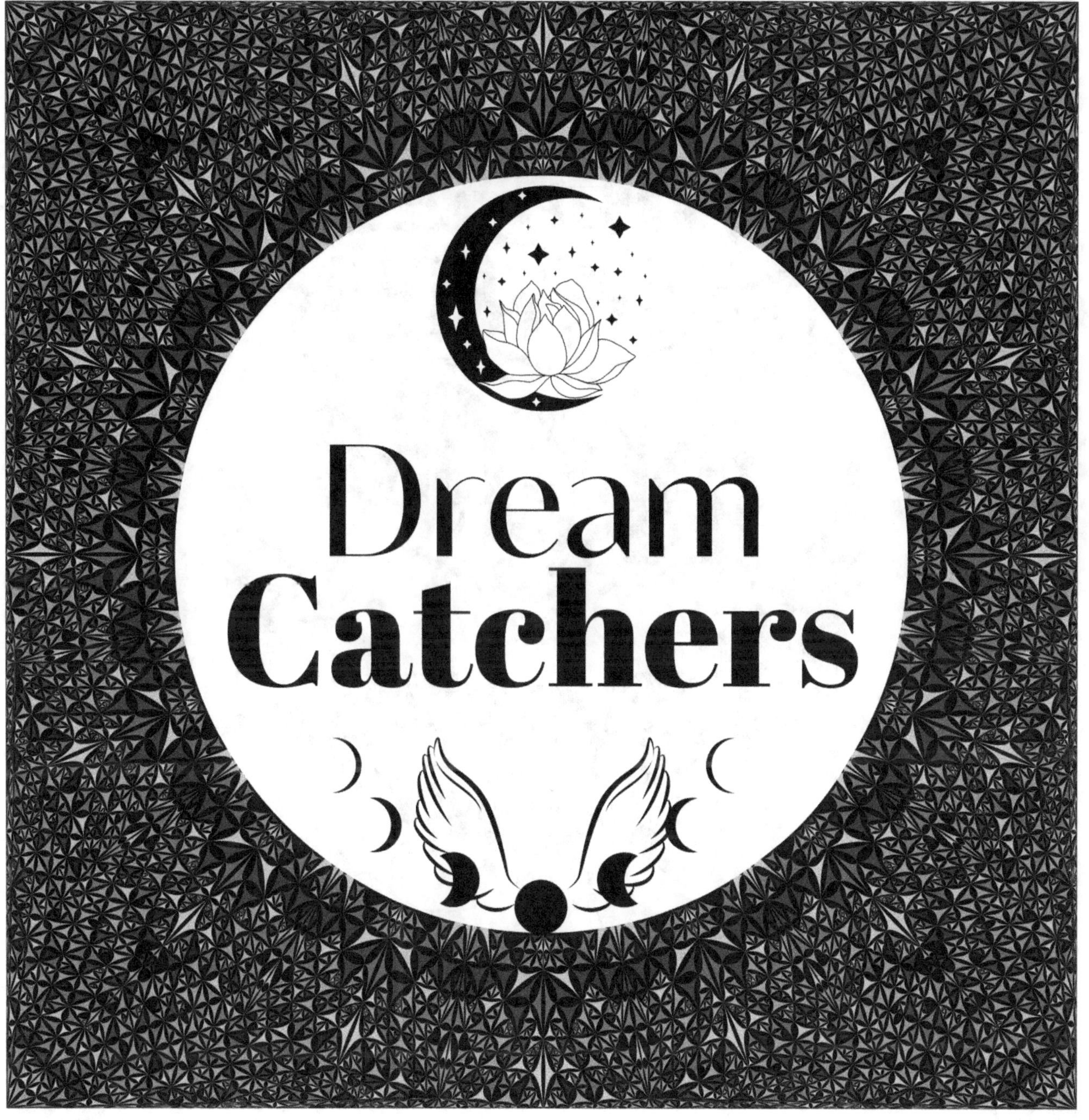
Dream
Catchers

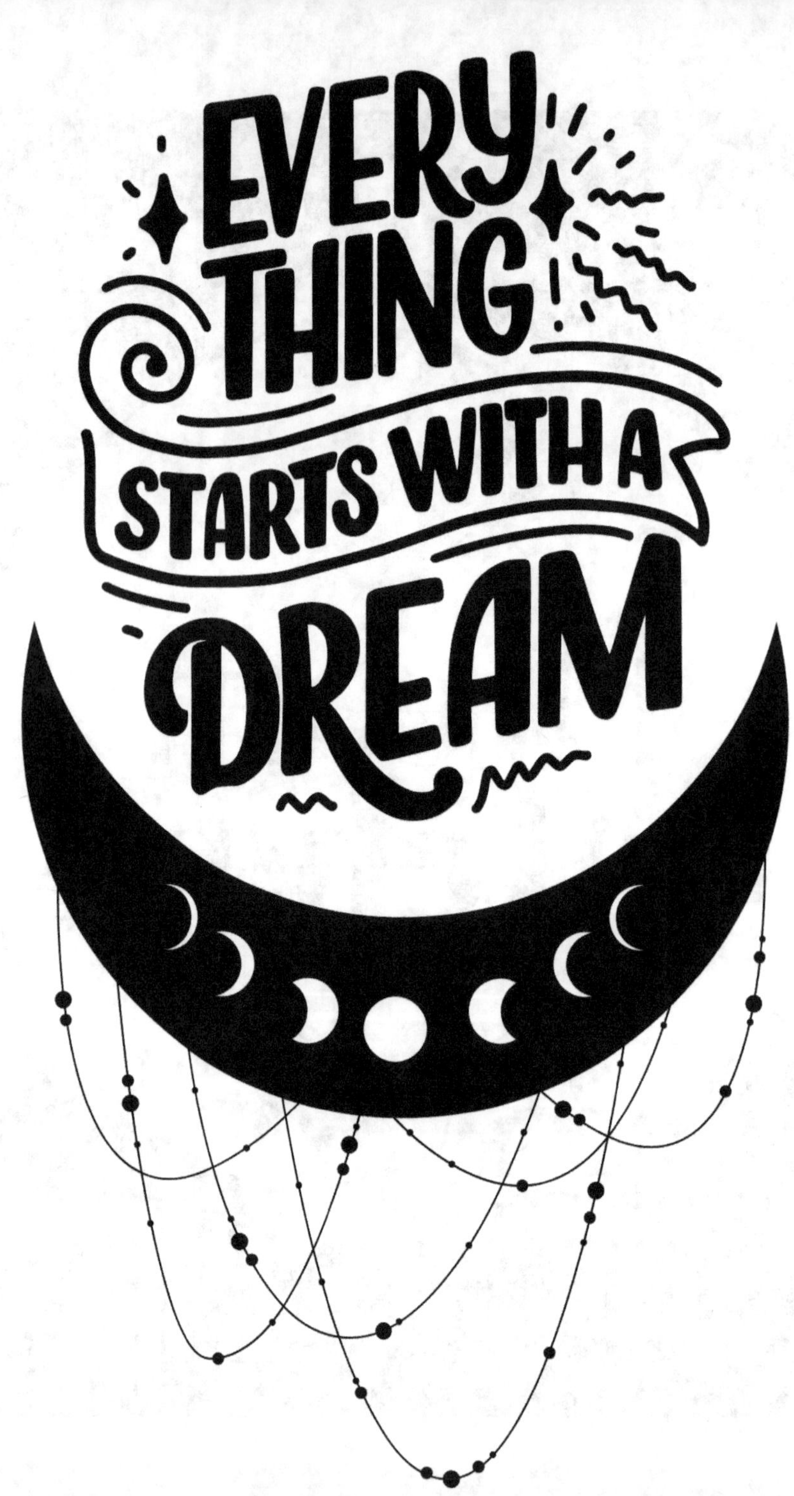
EVERY
THING
STARTS WITH A
DREAM

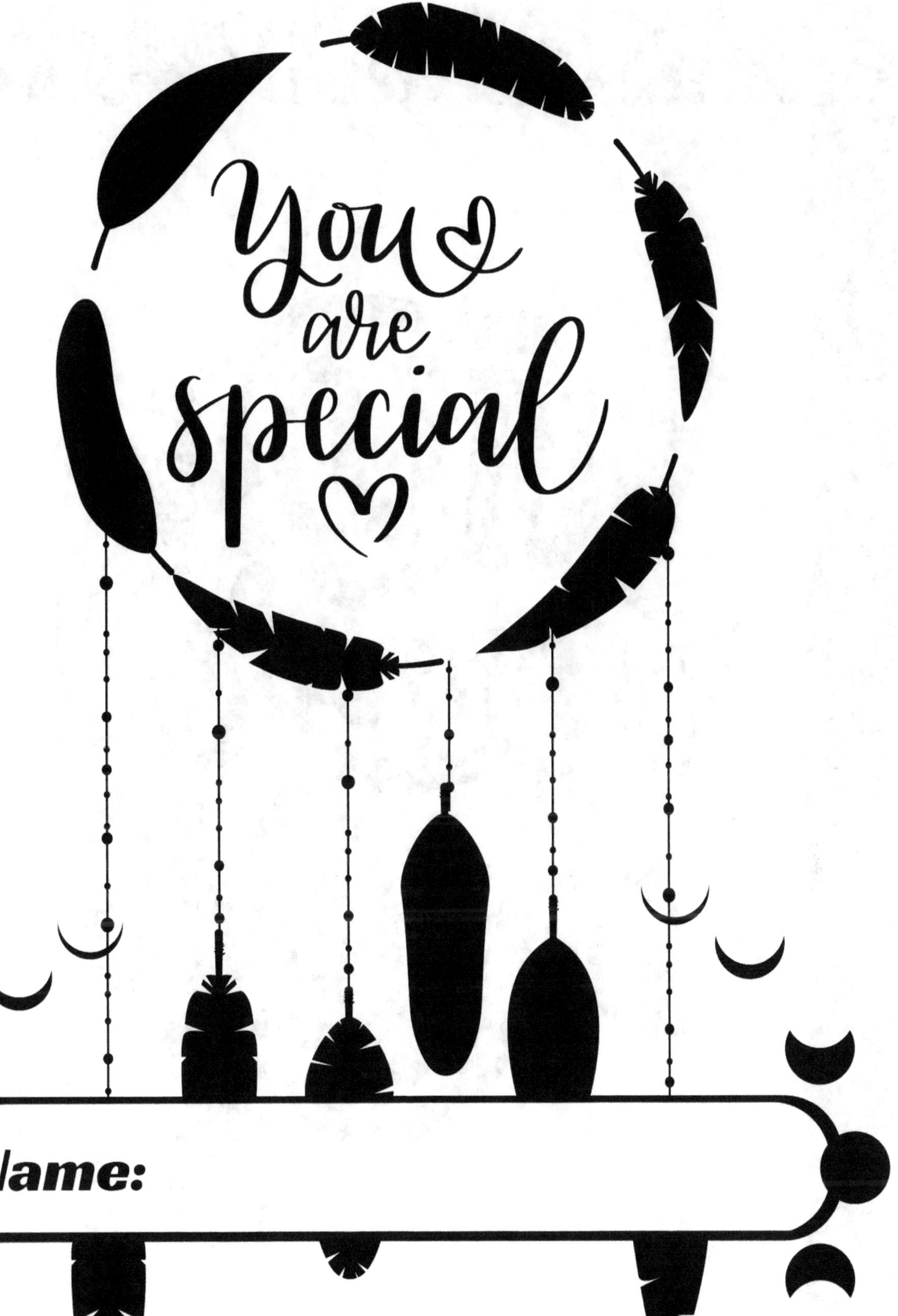
You
are
special

Name:

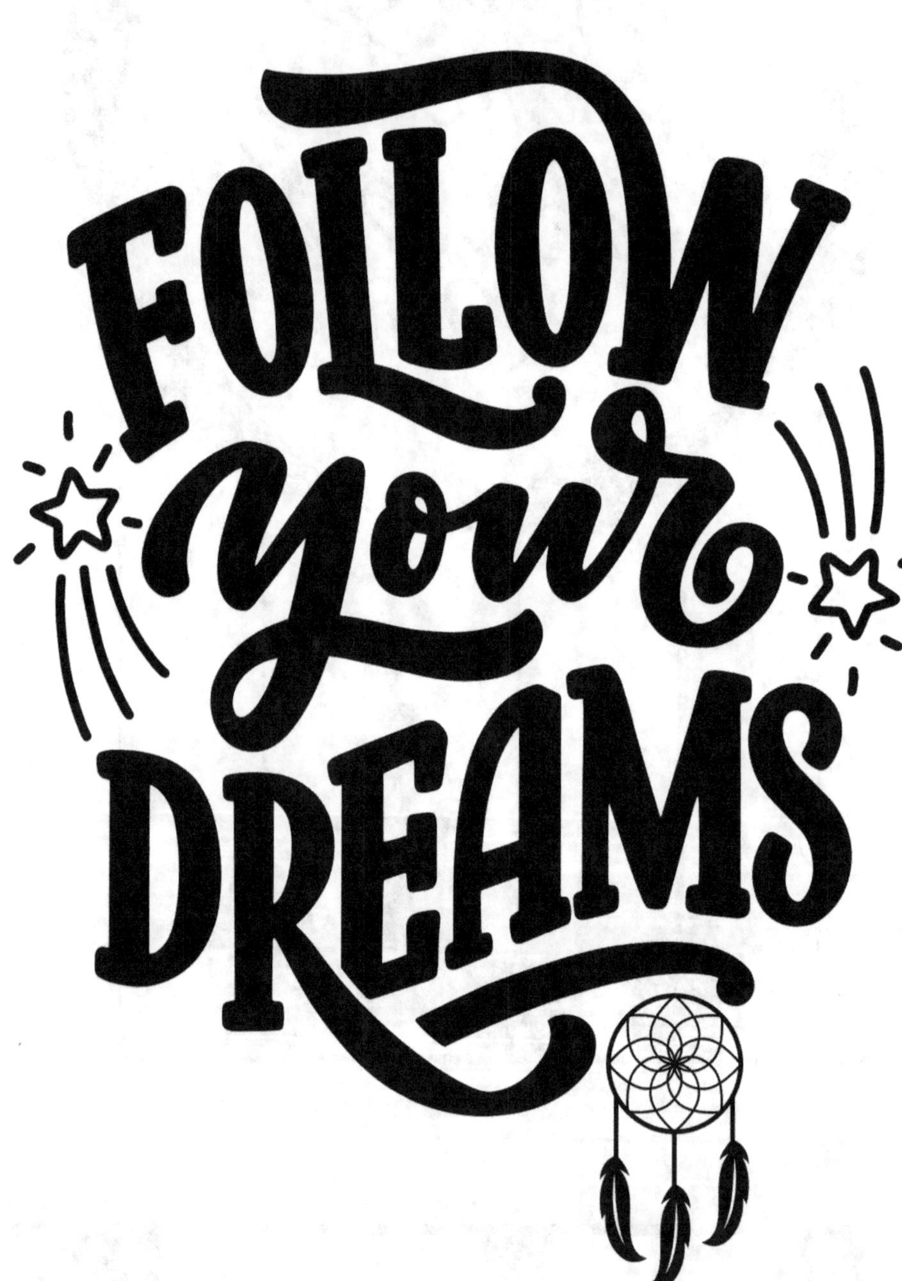

FOLLOW
YOUR
DREAMS

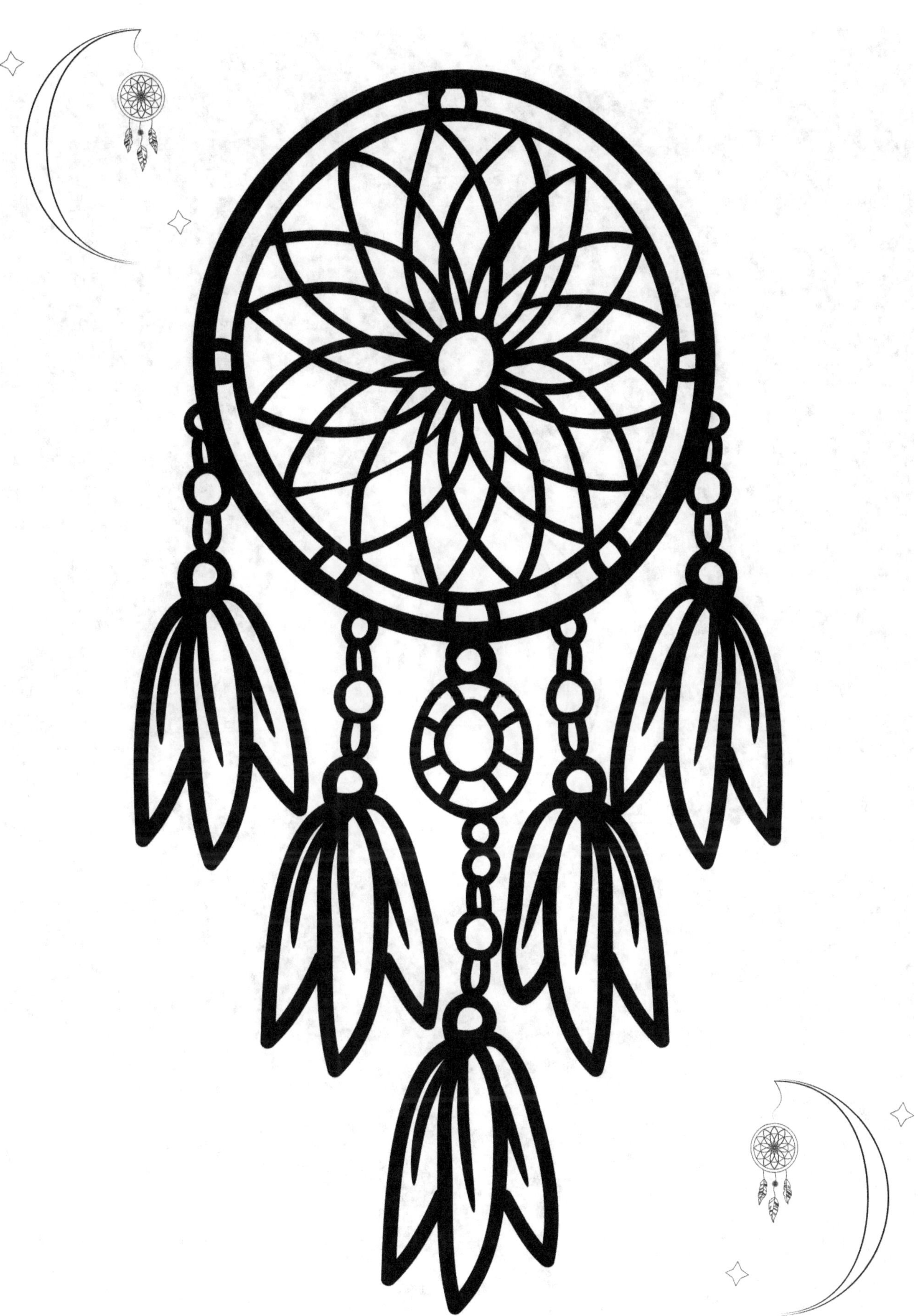

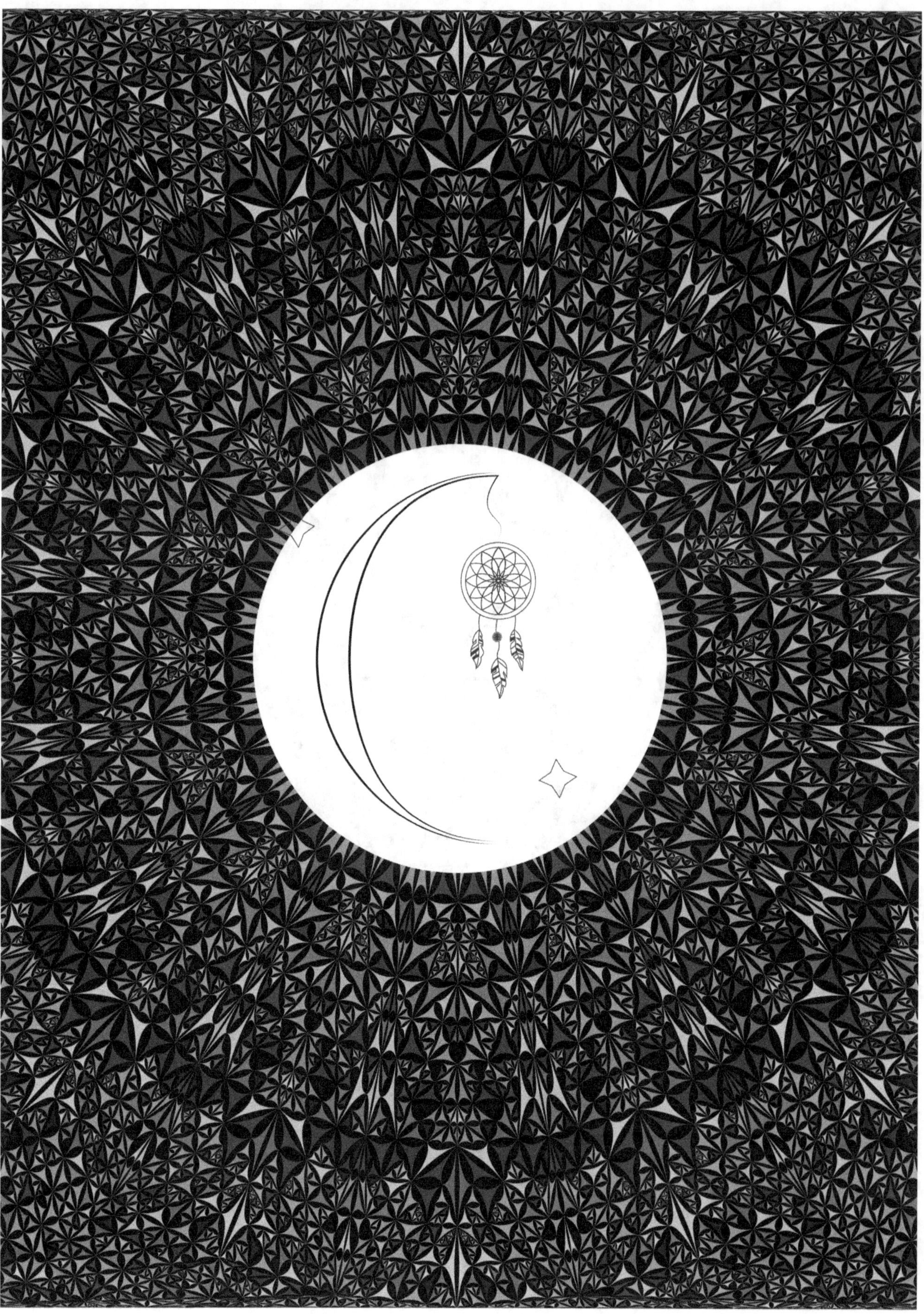

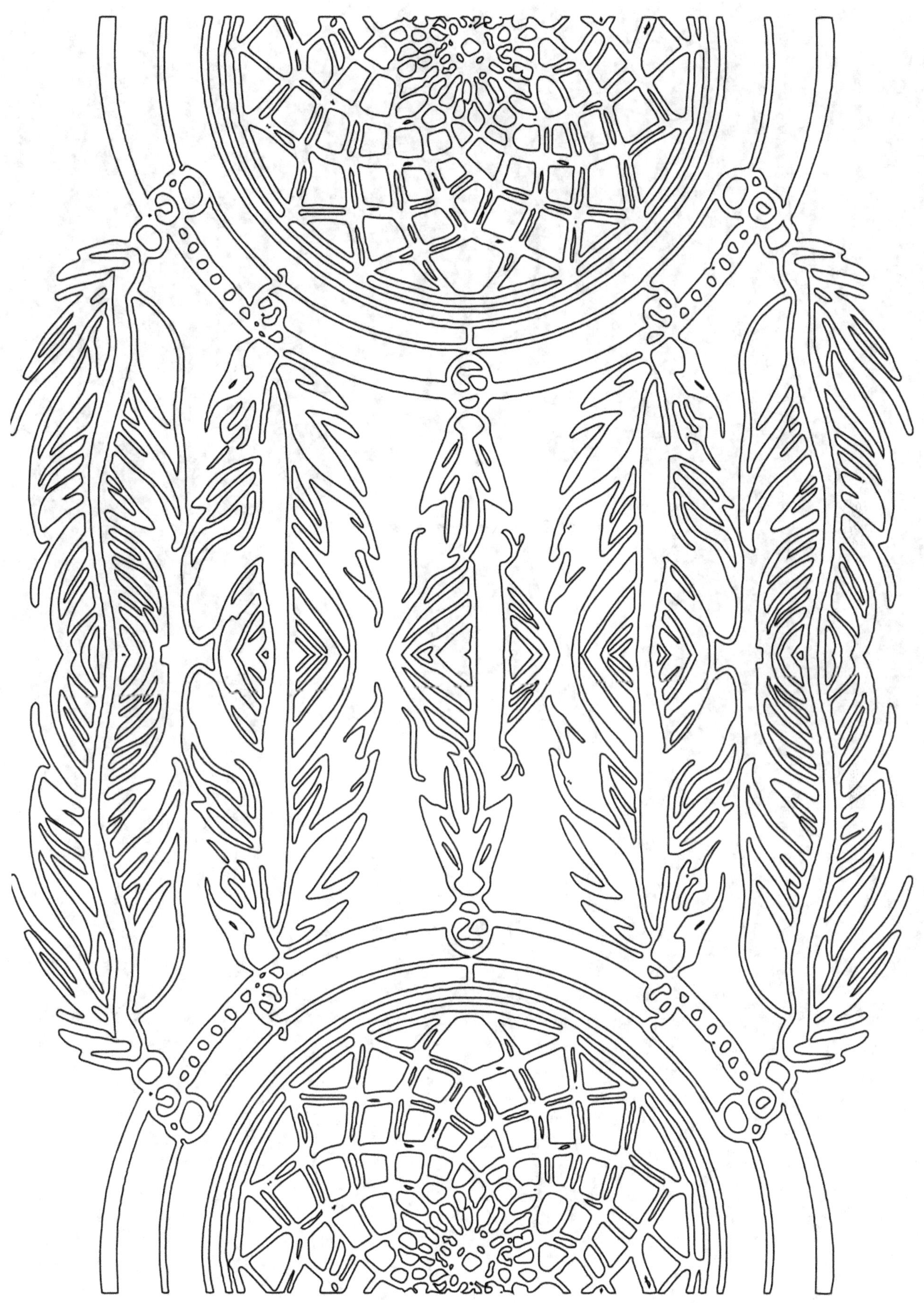

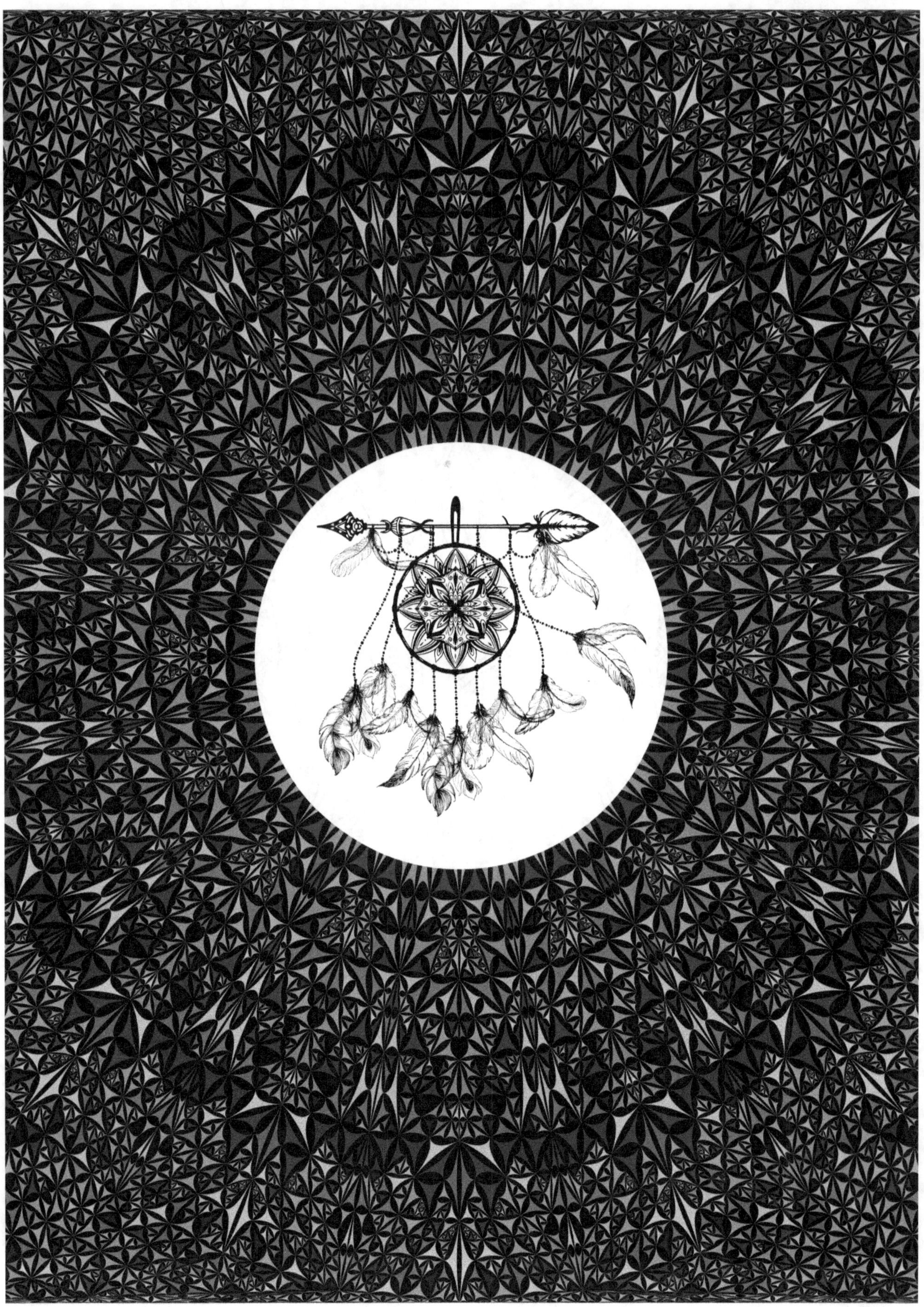

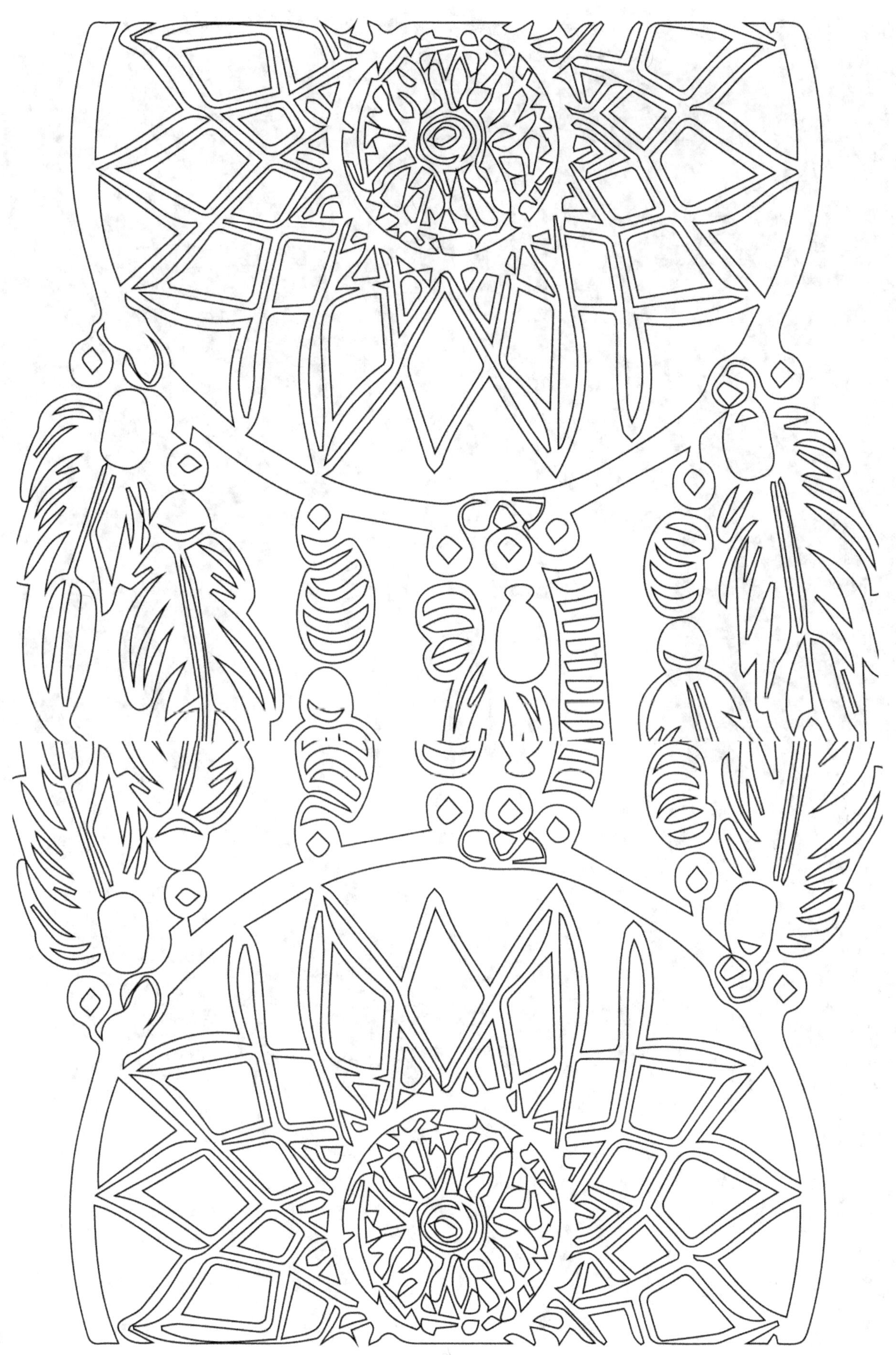

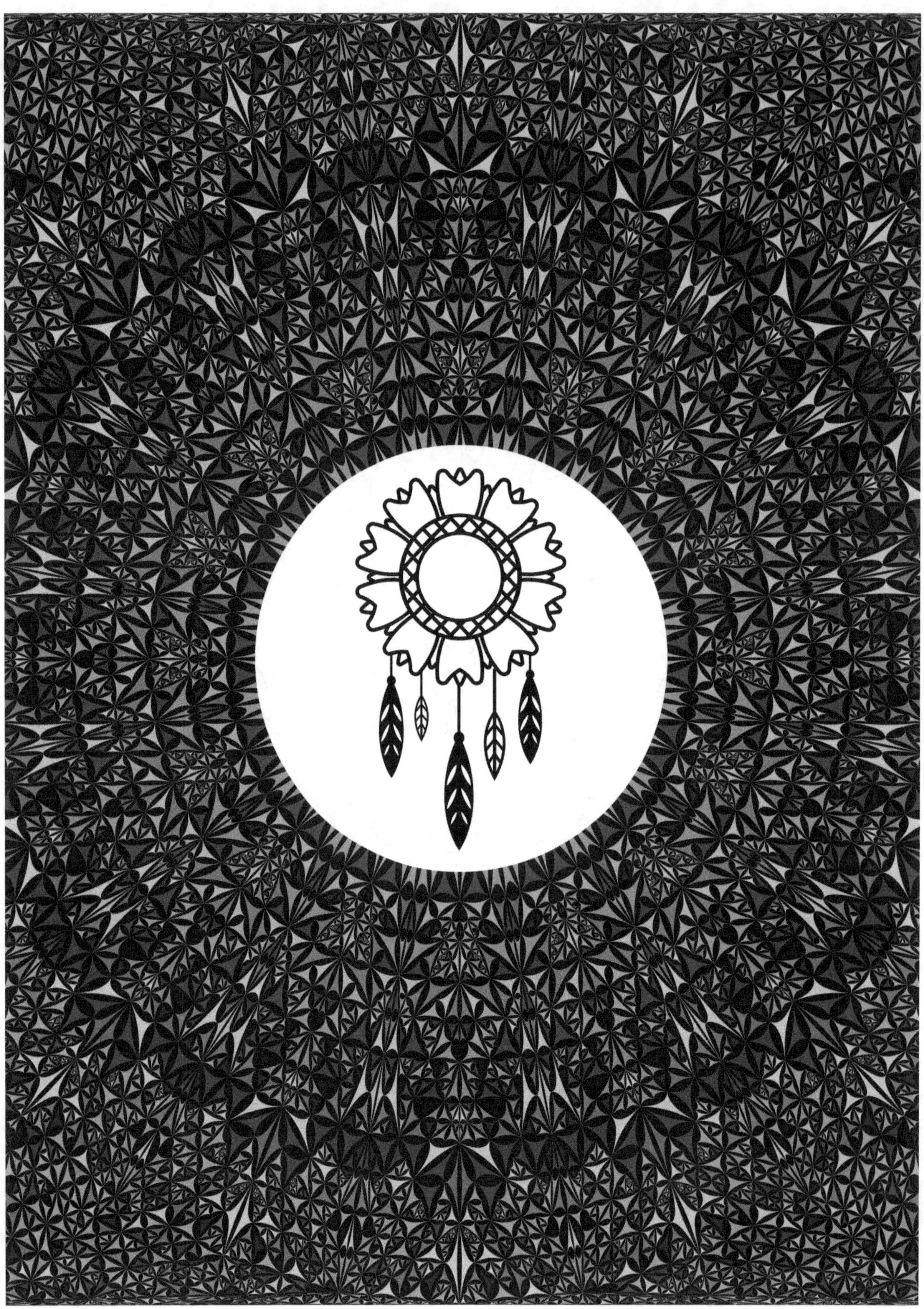

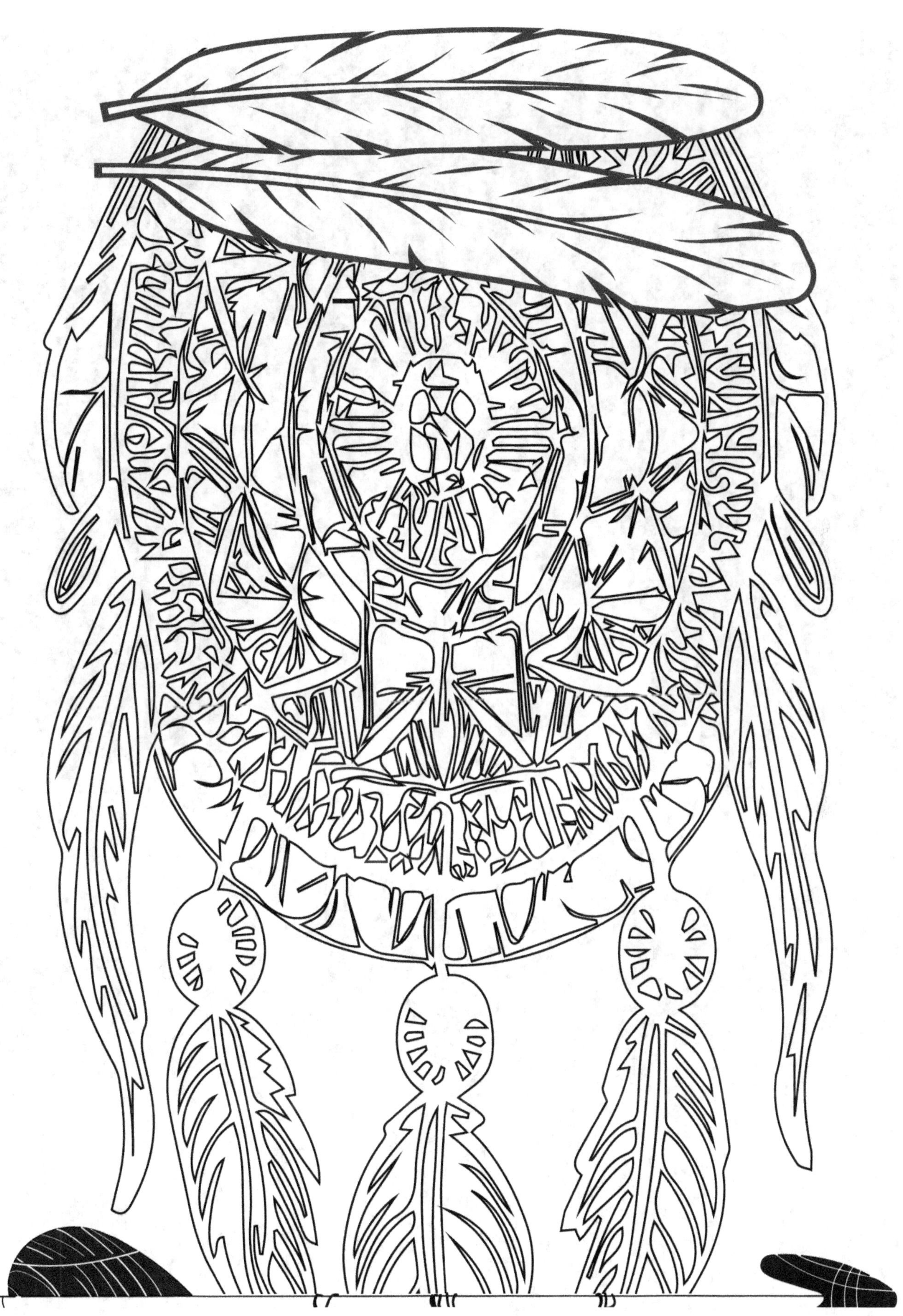

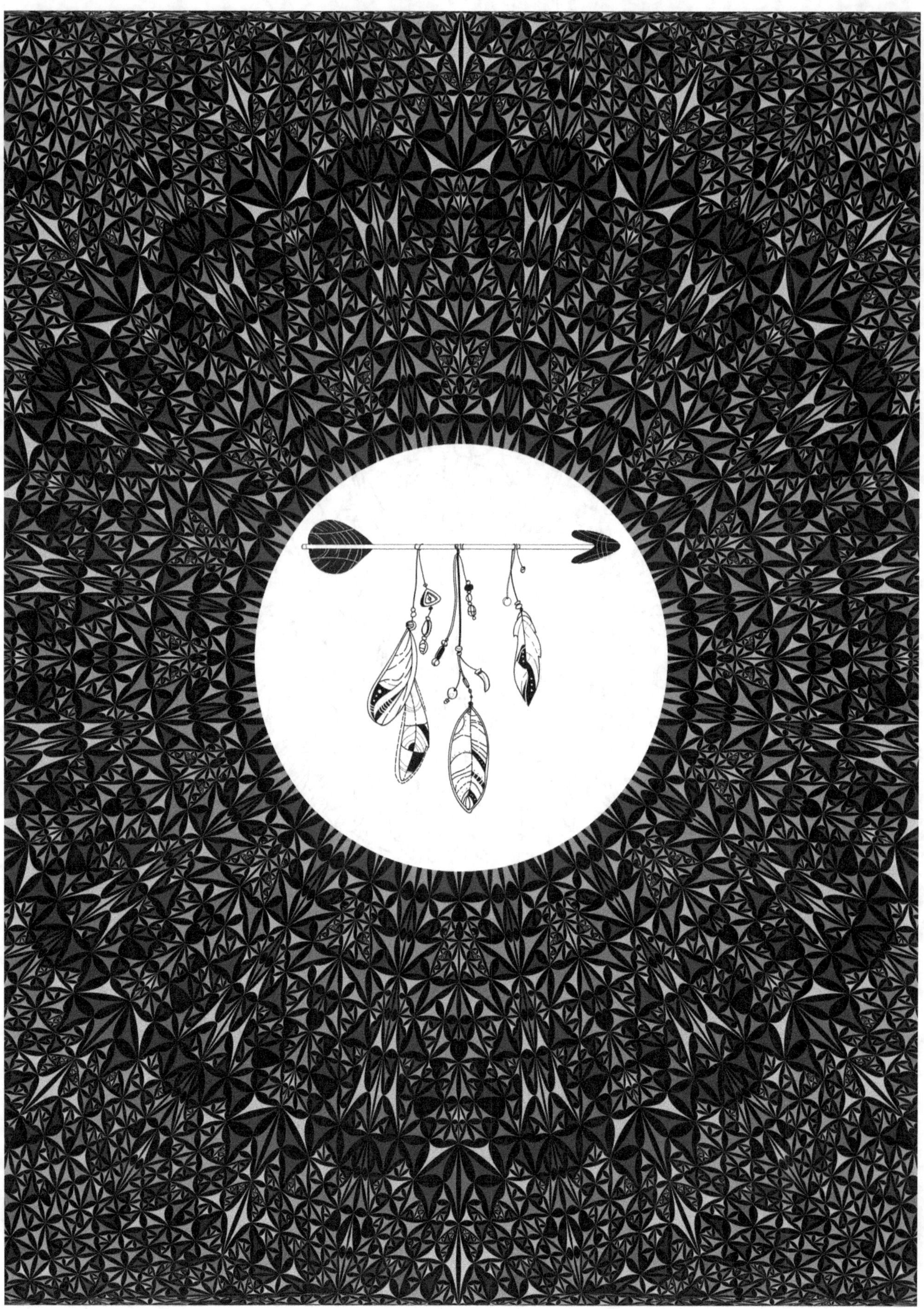

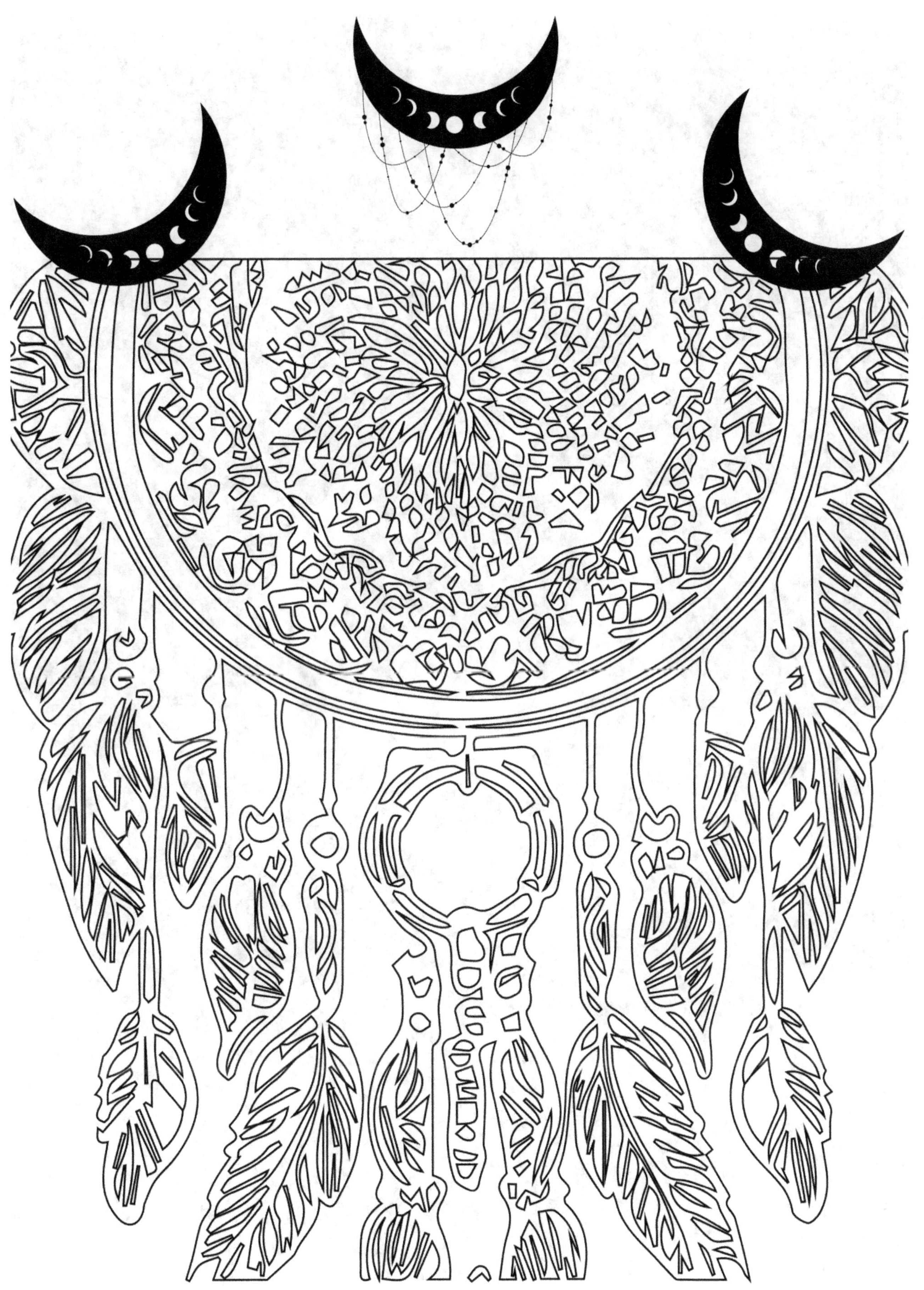

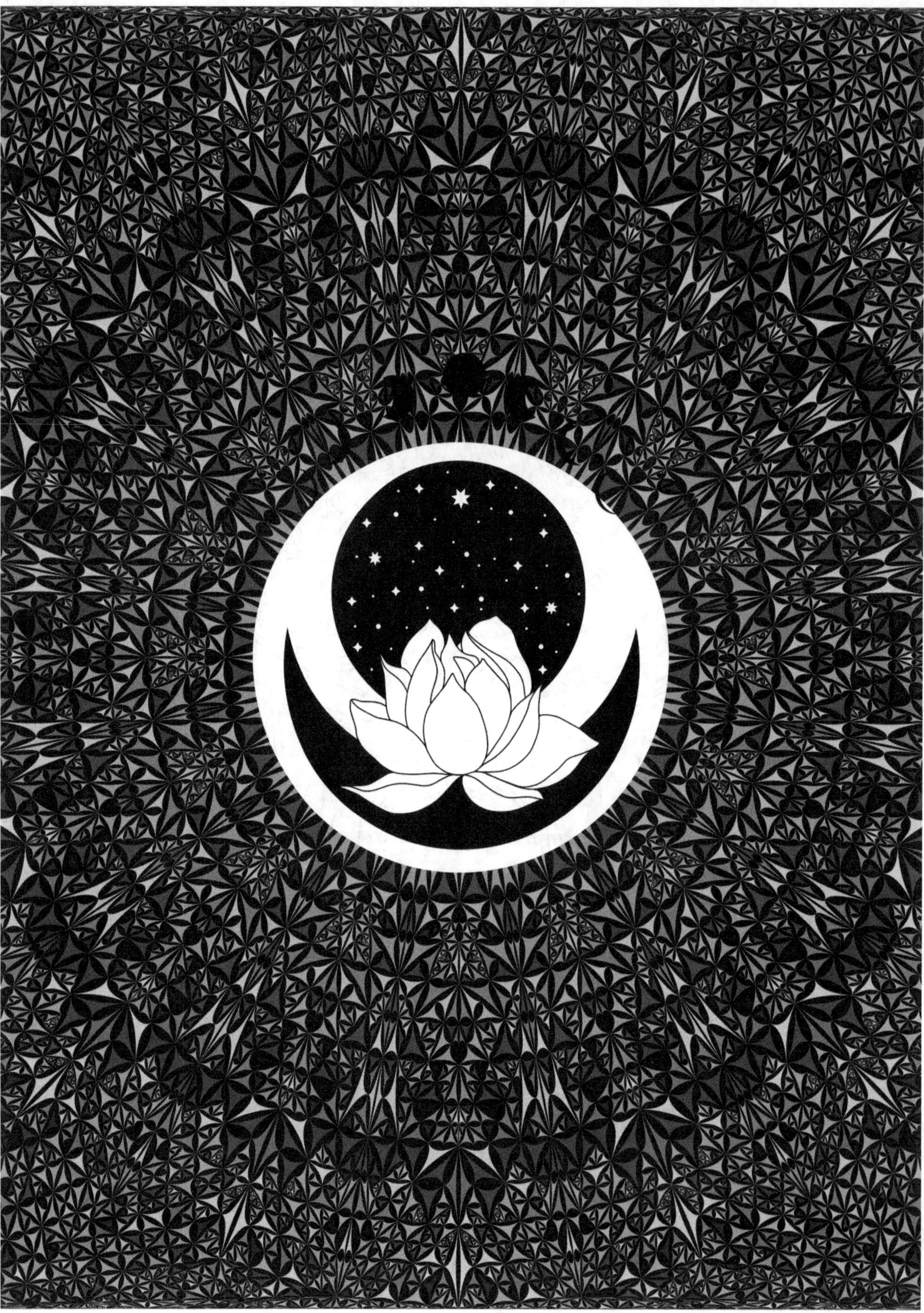

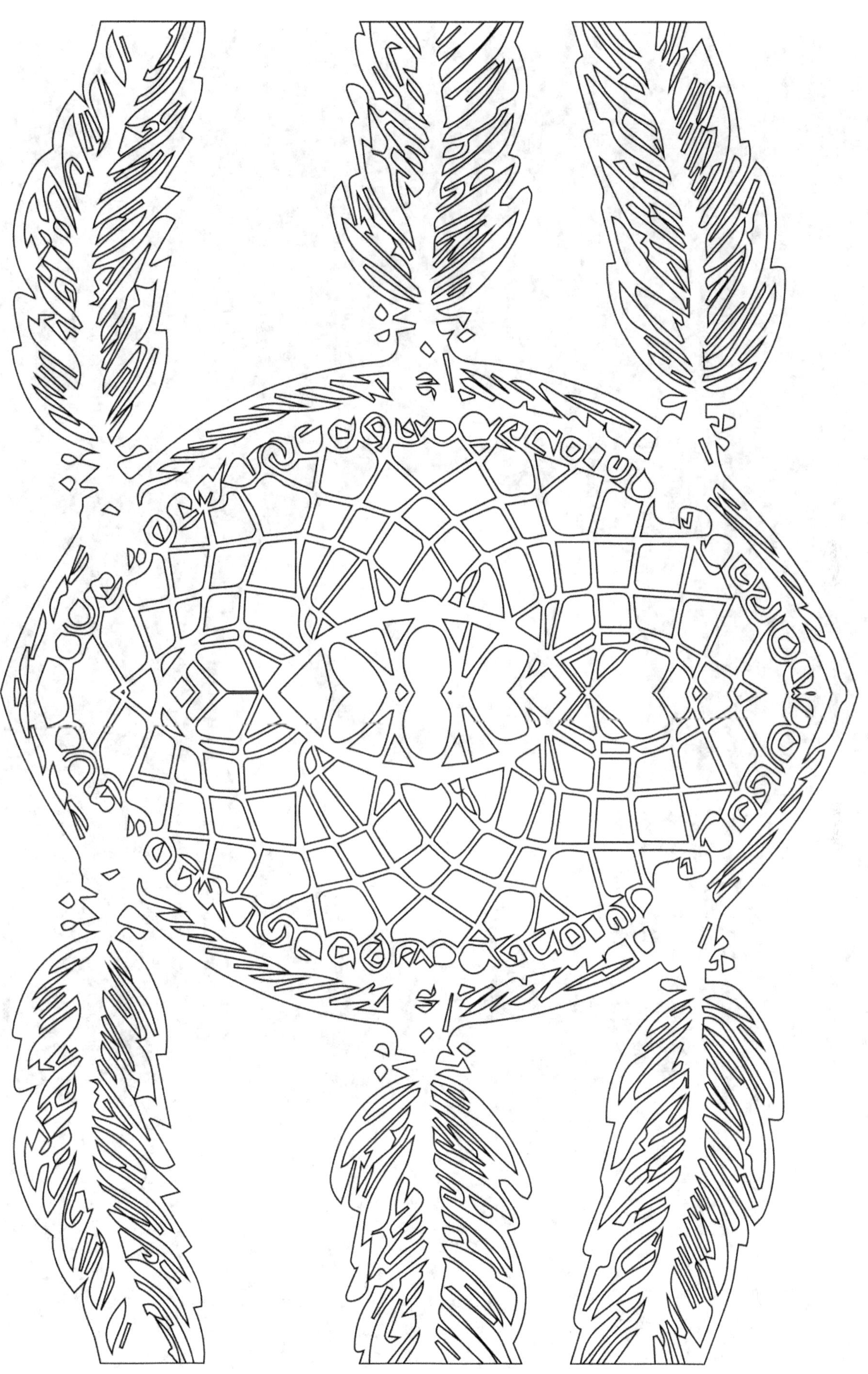

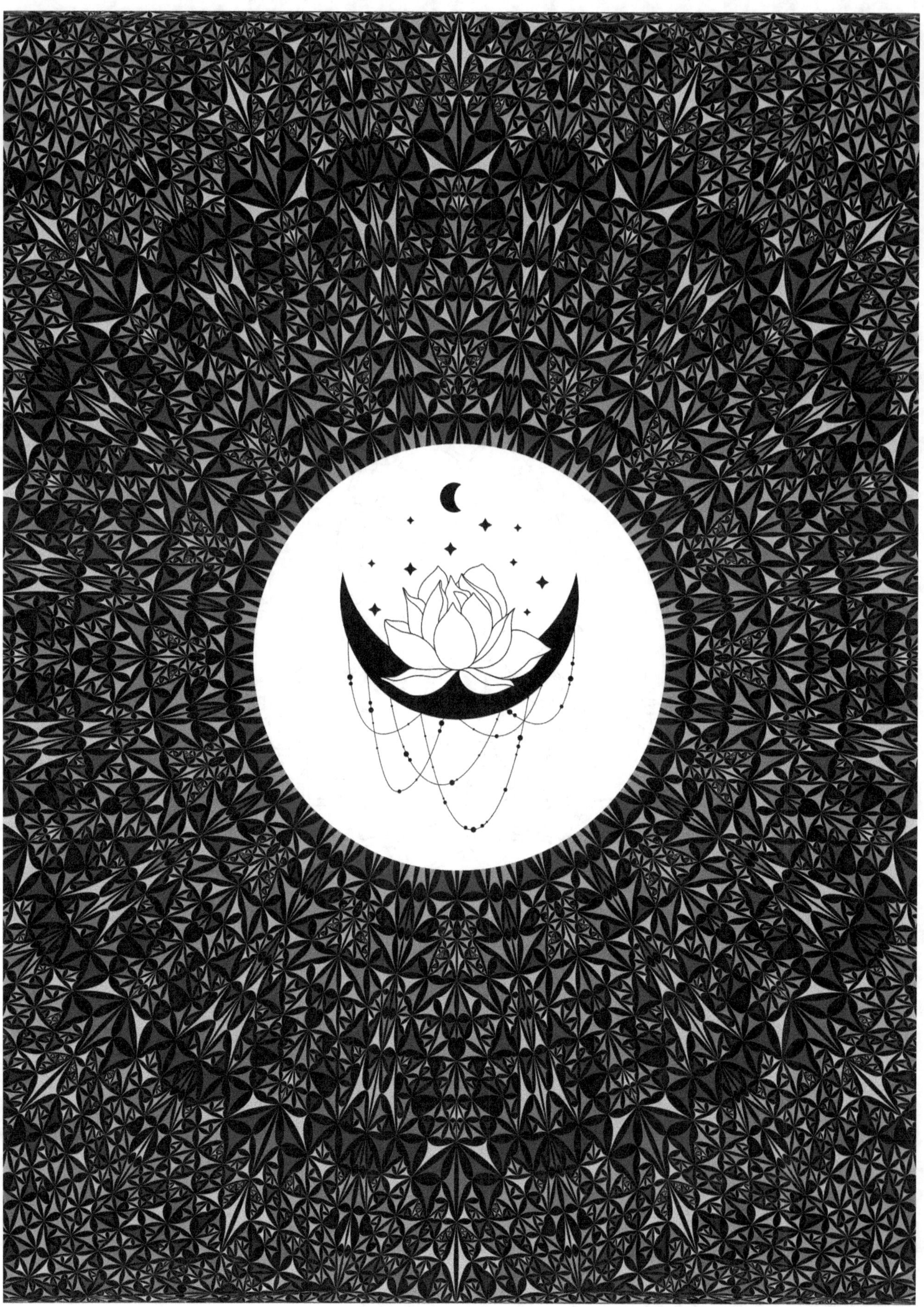

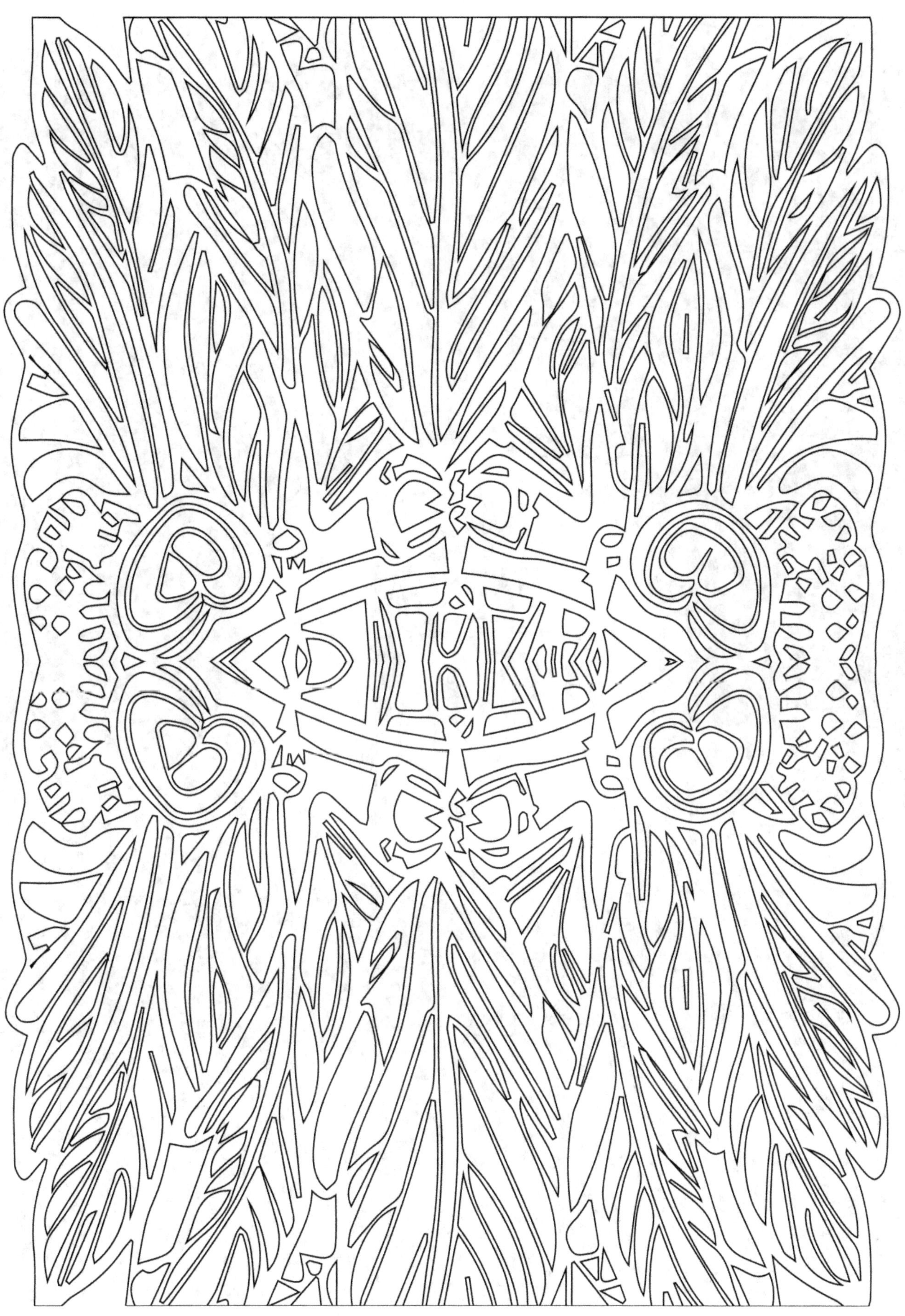

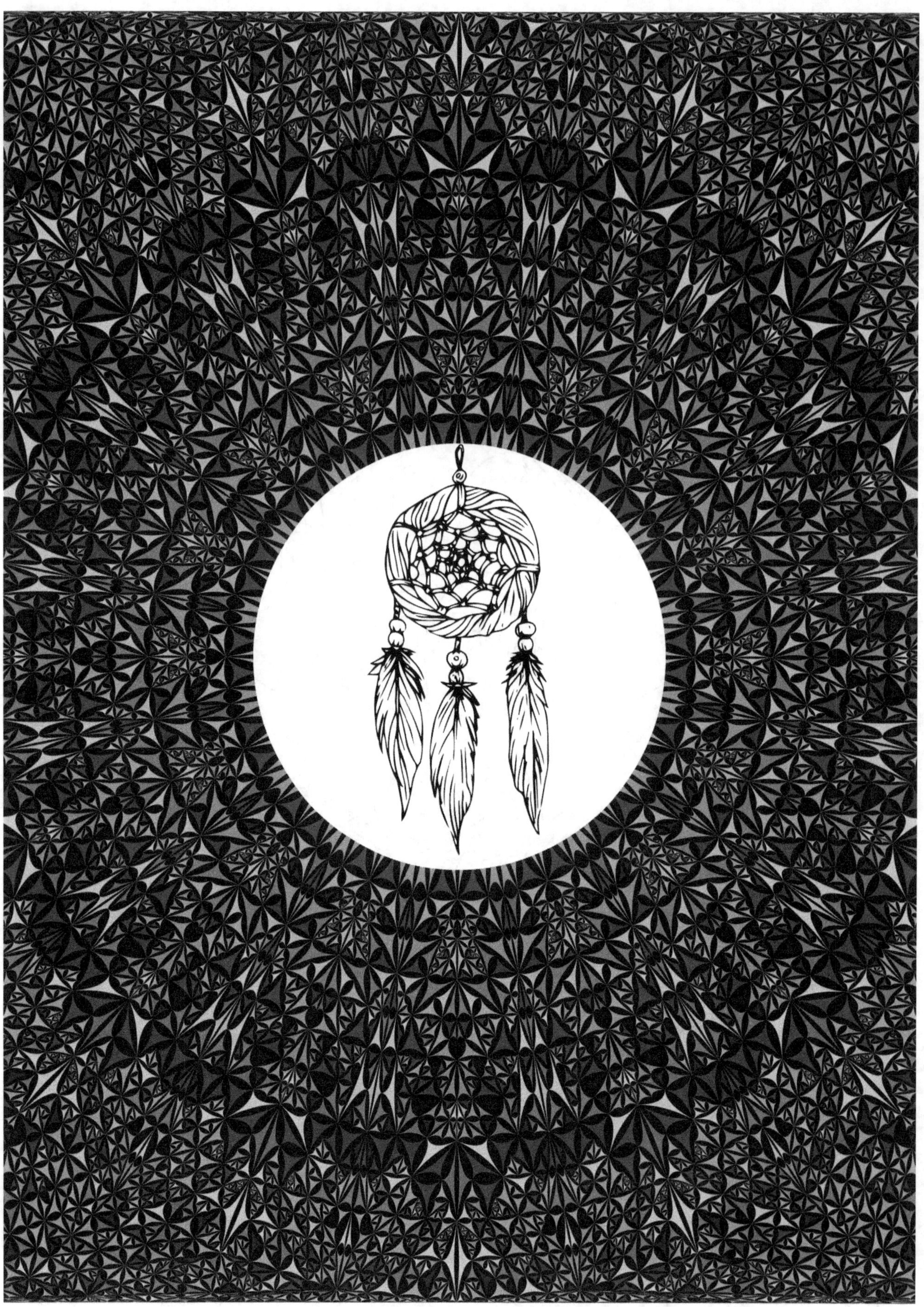

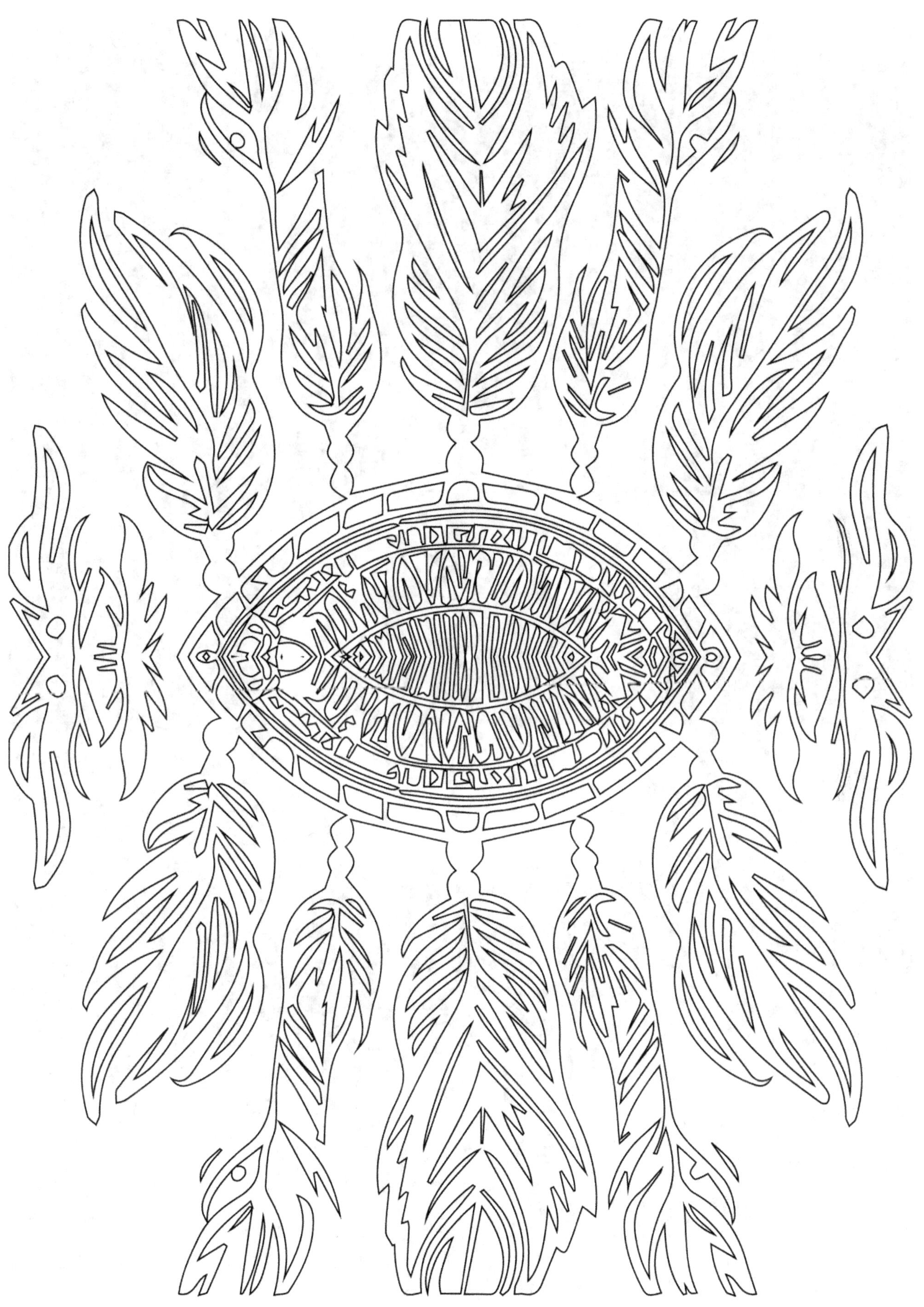

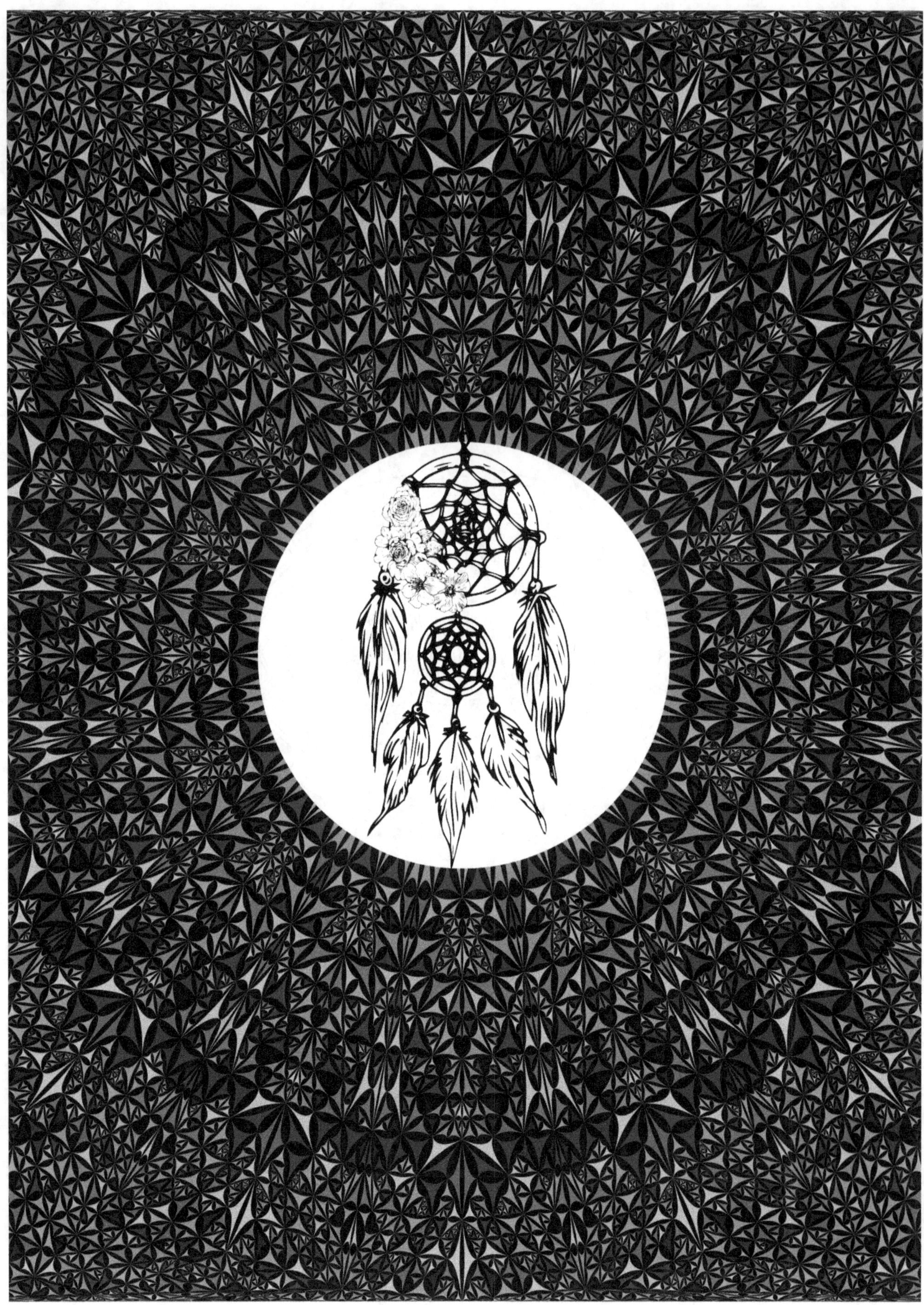

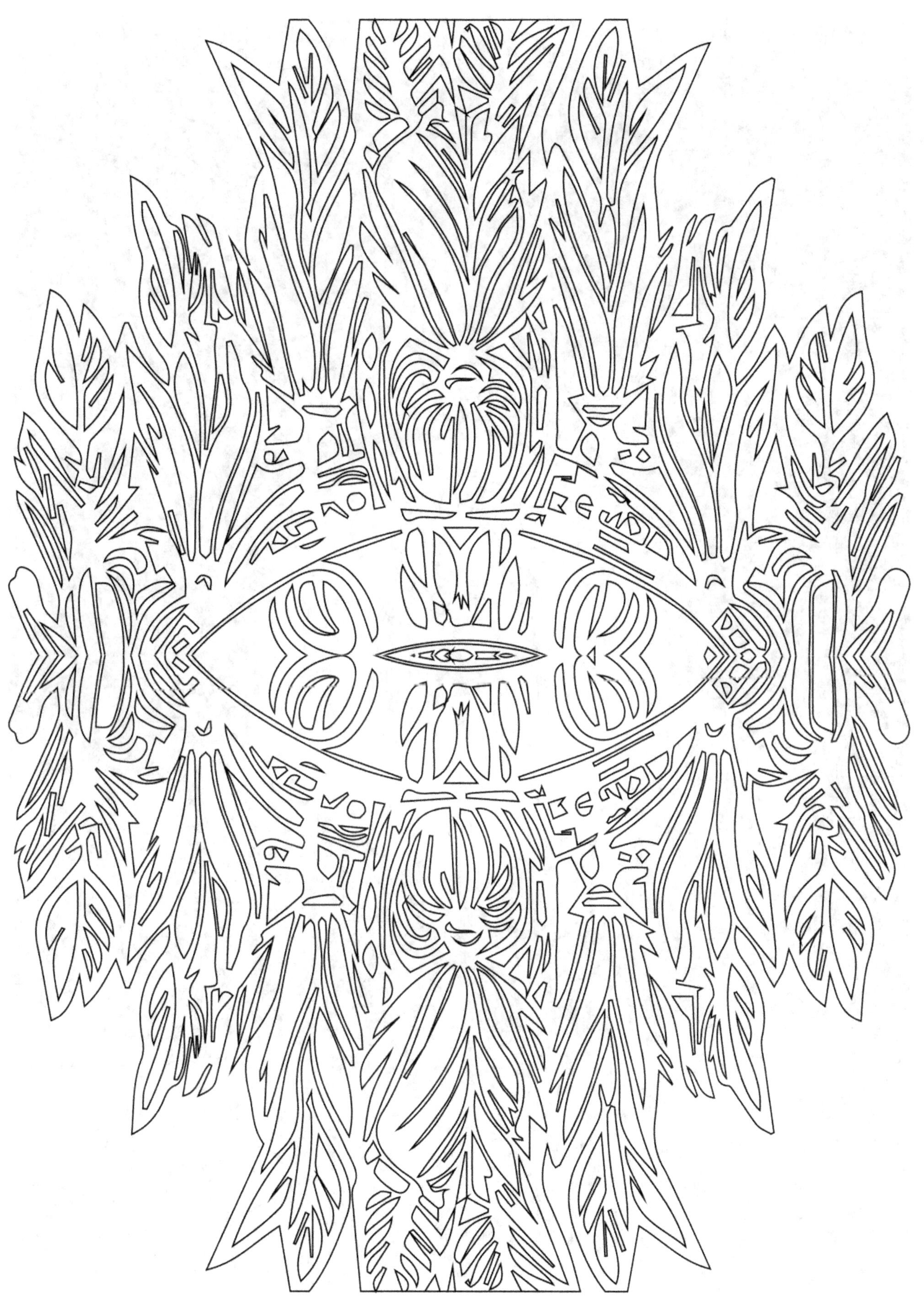

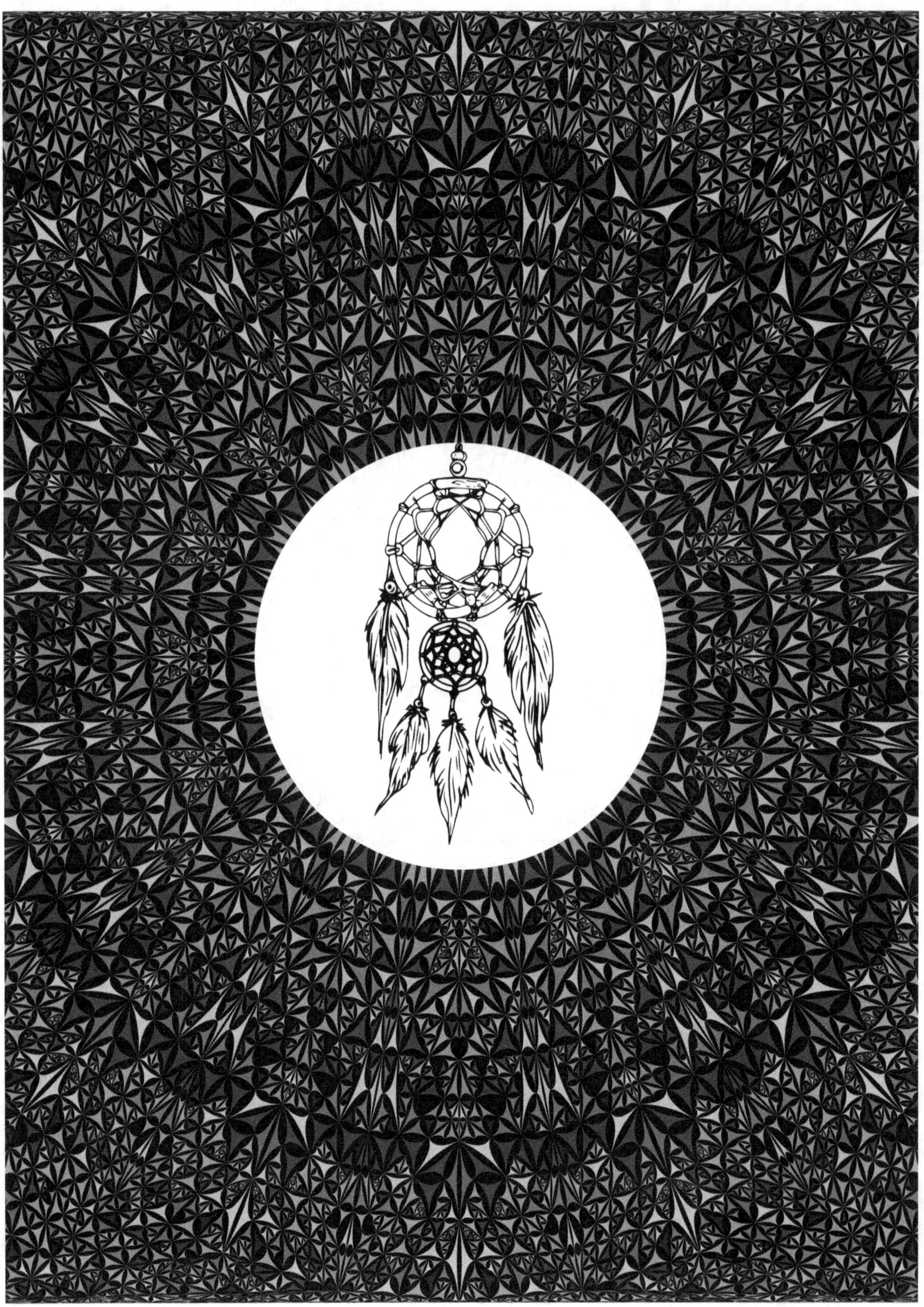

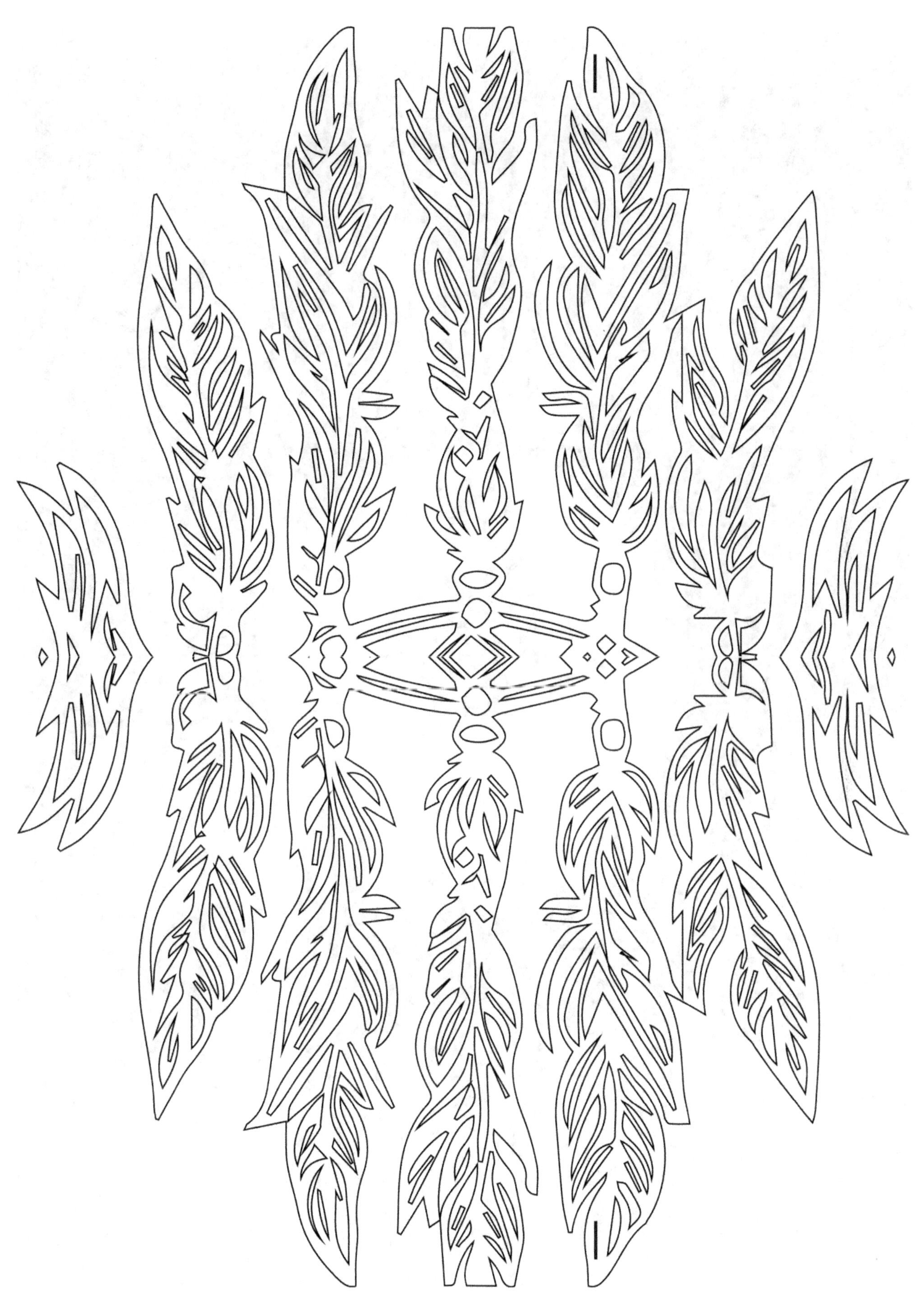

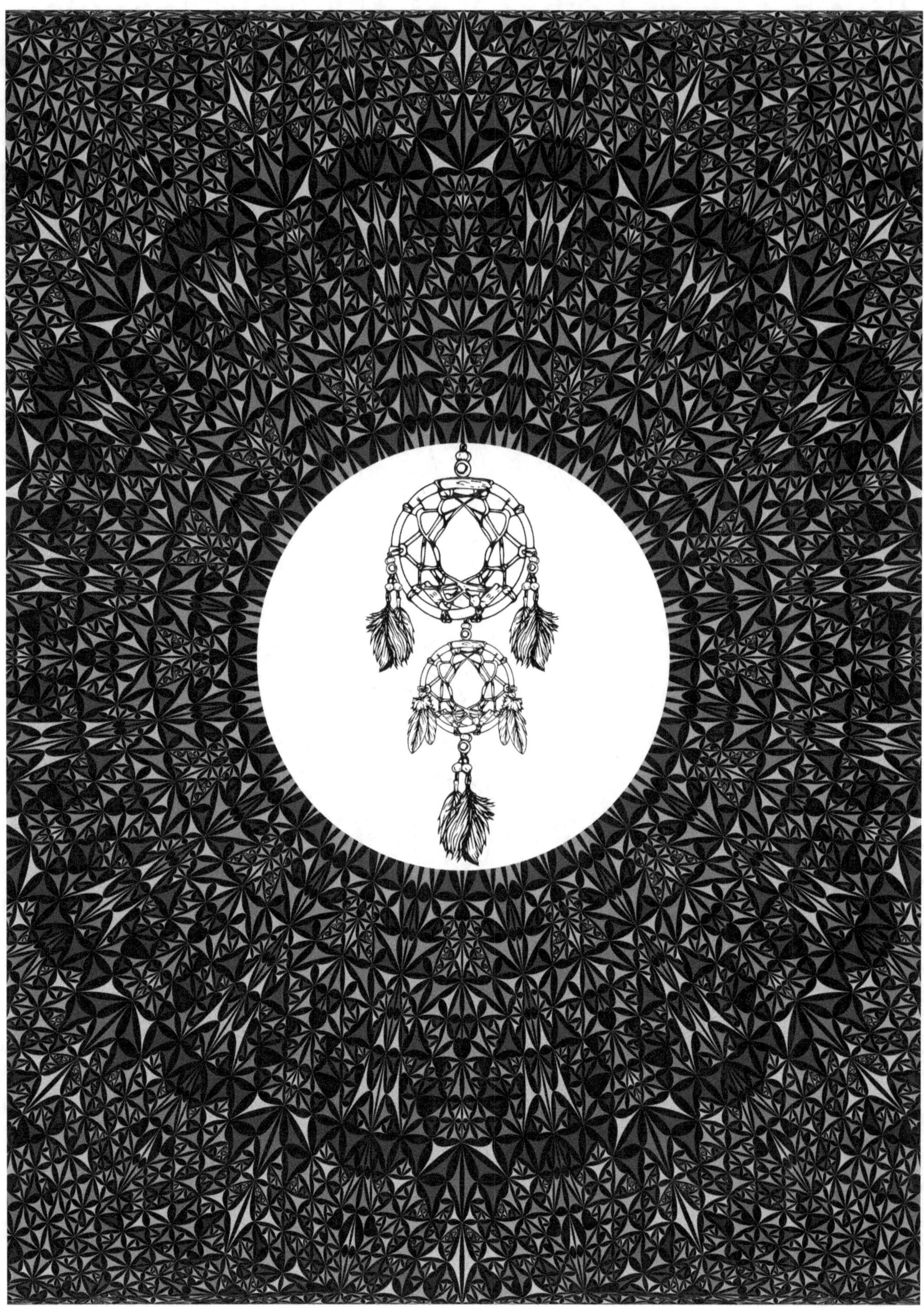

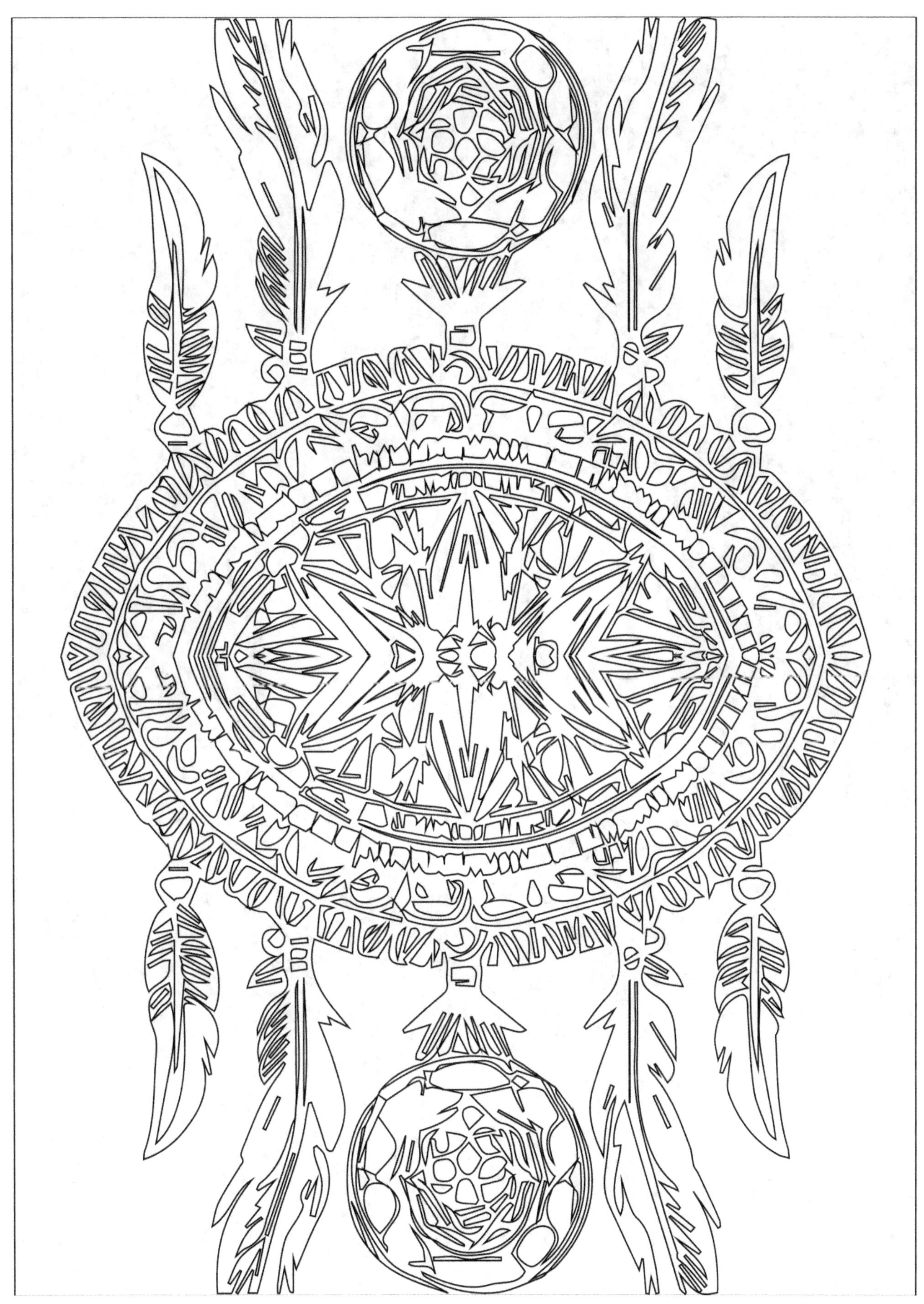

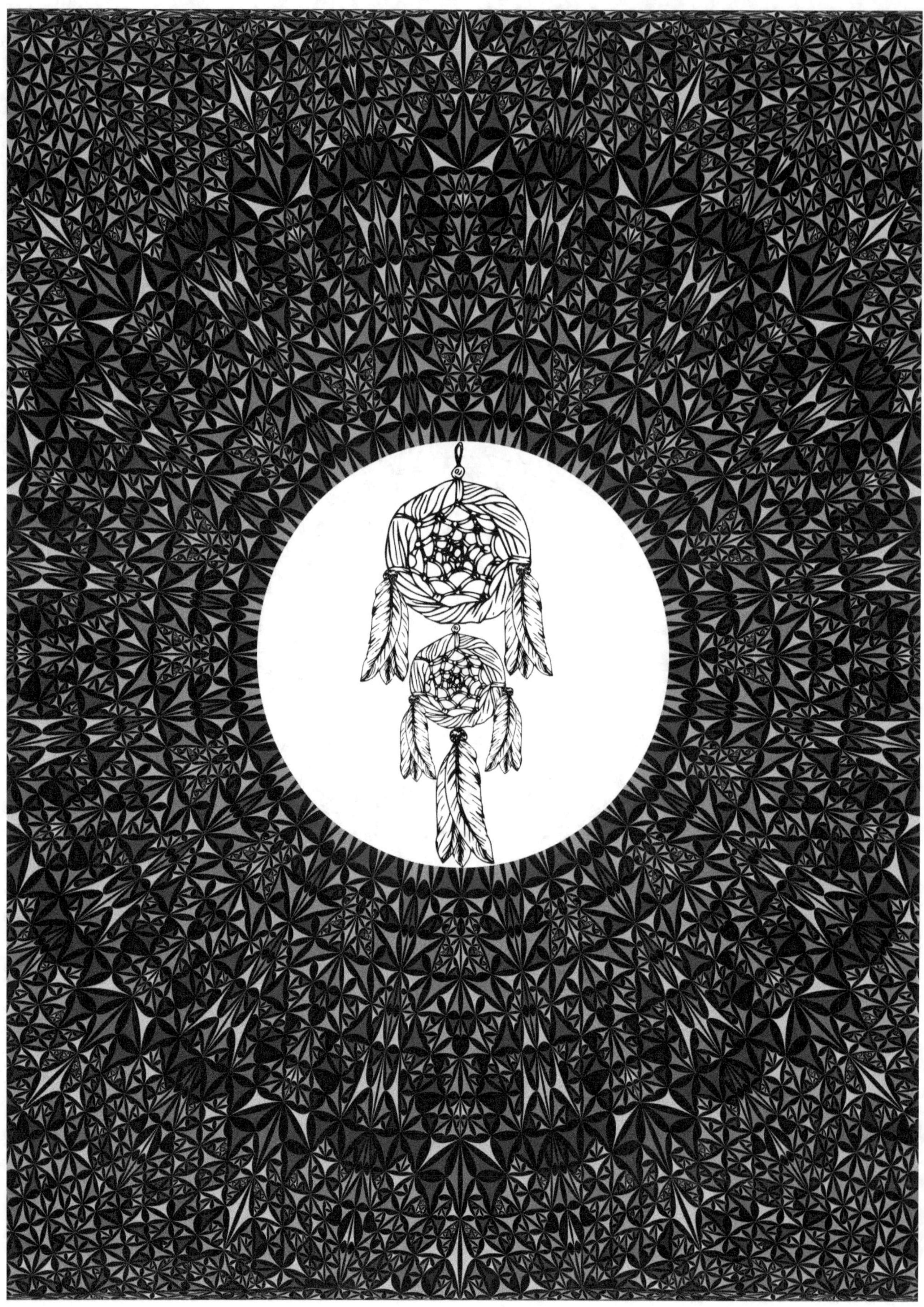

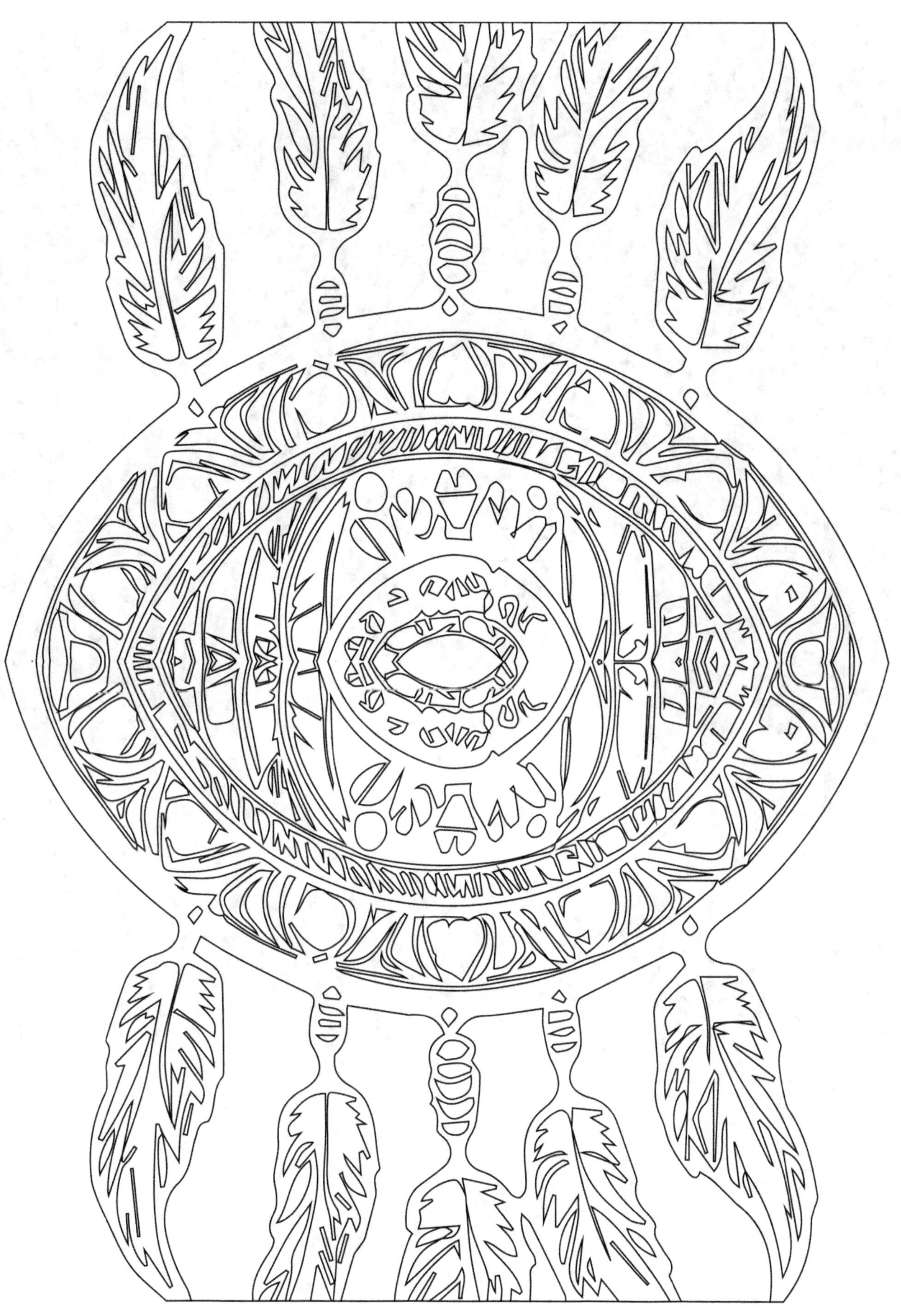

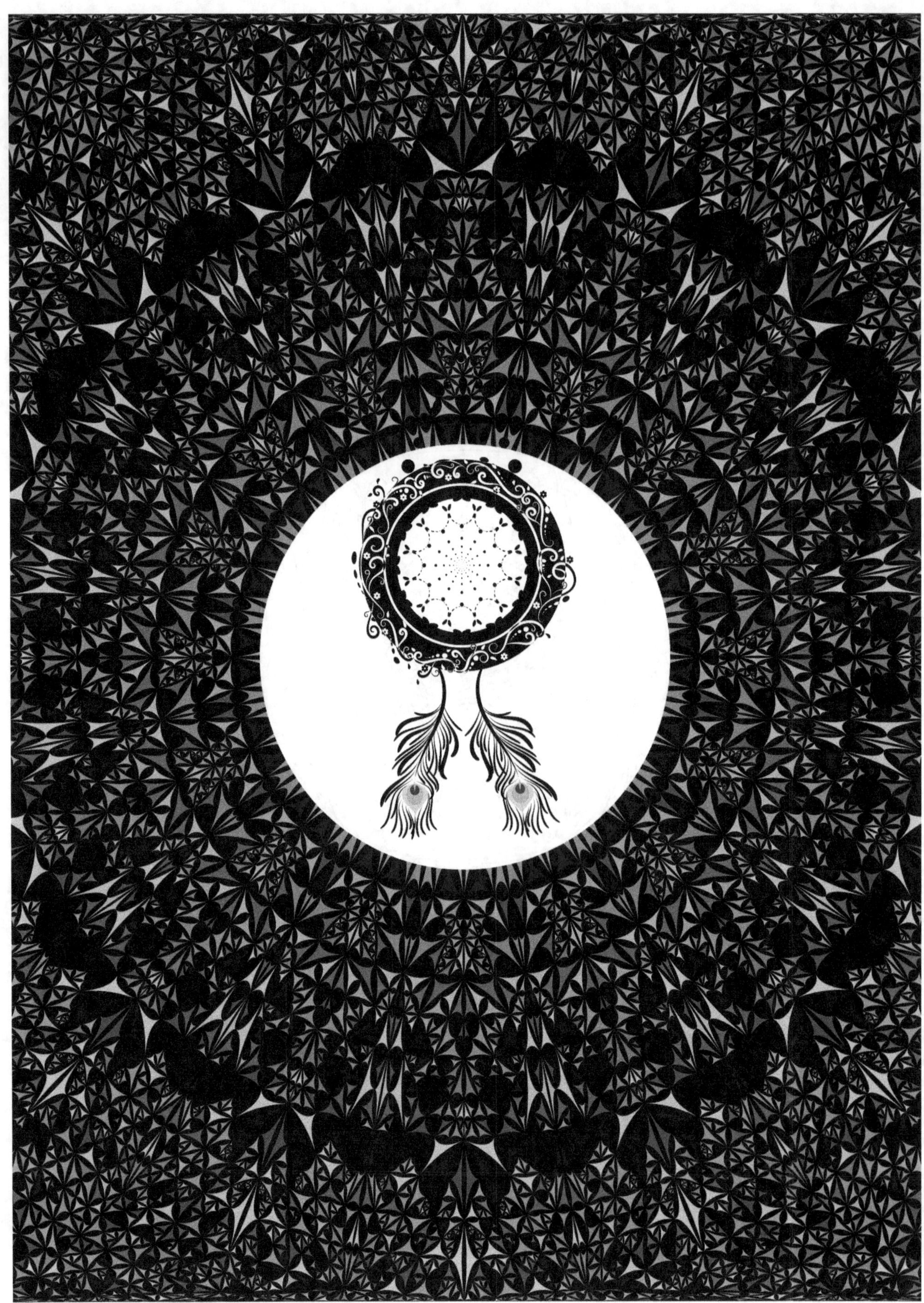

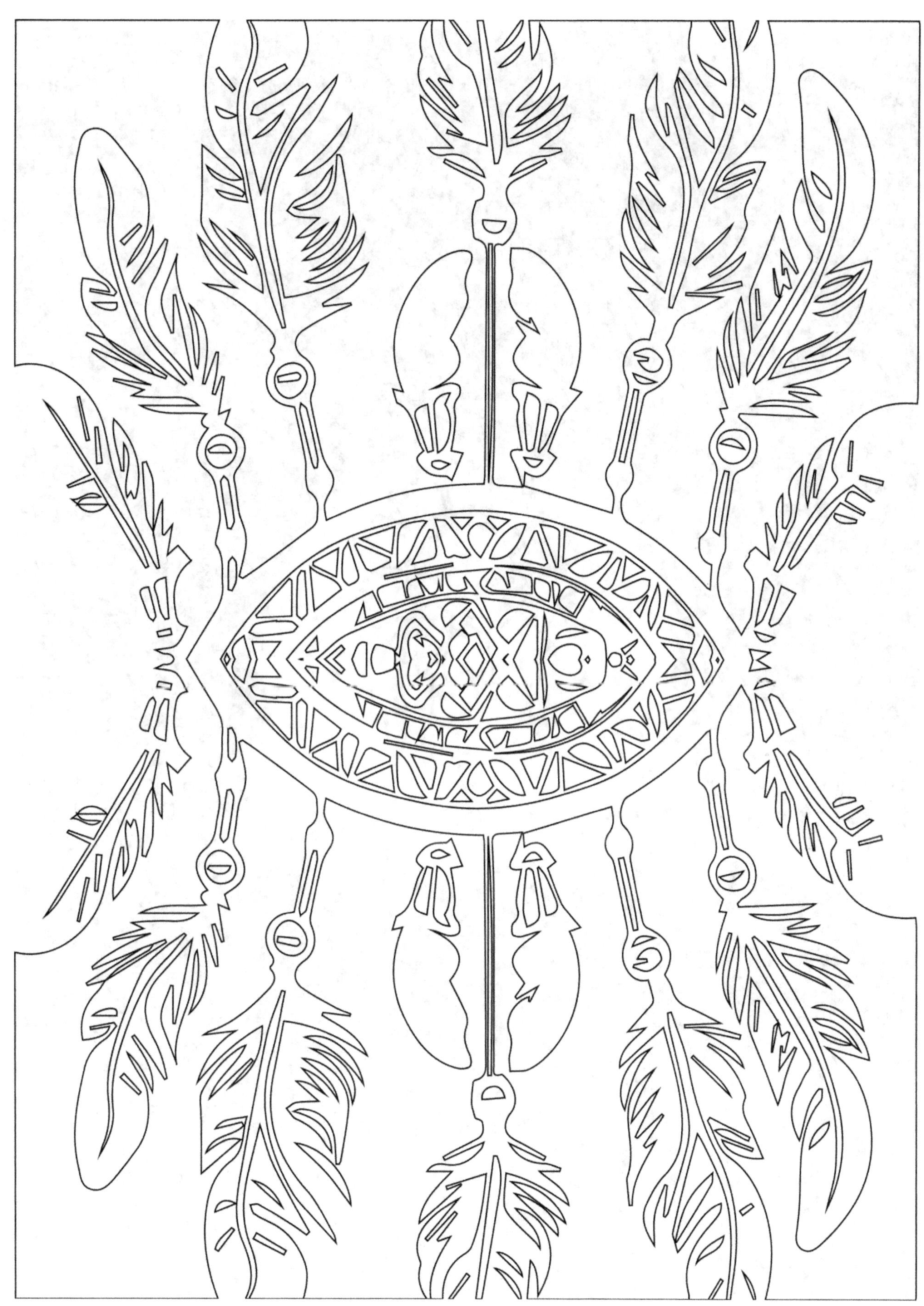

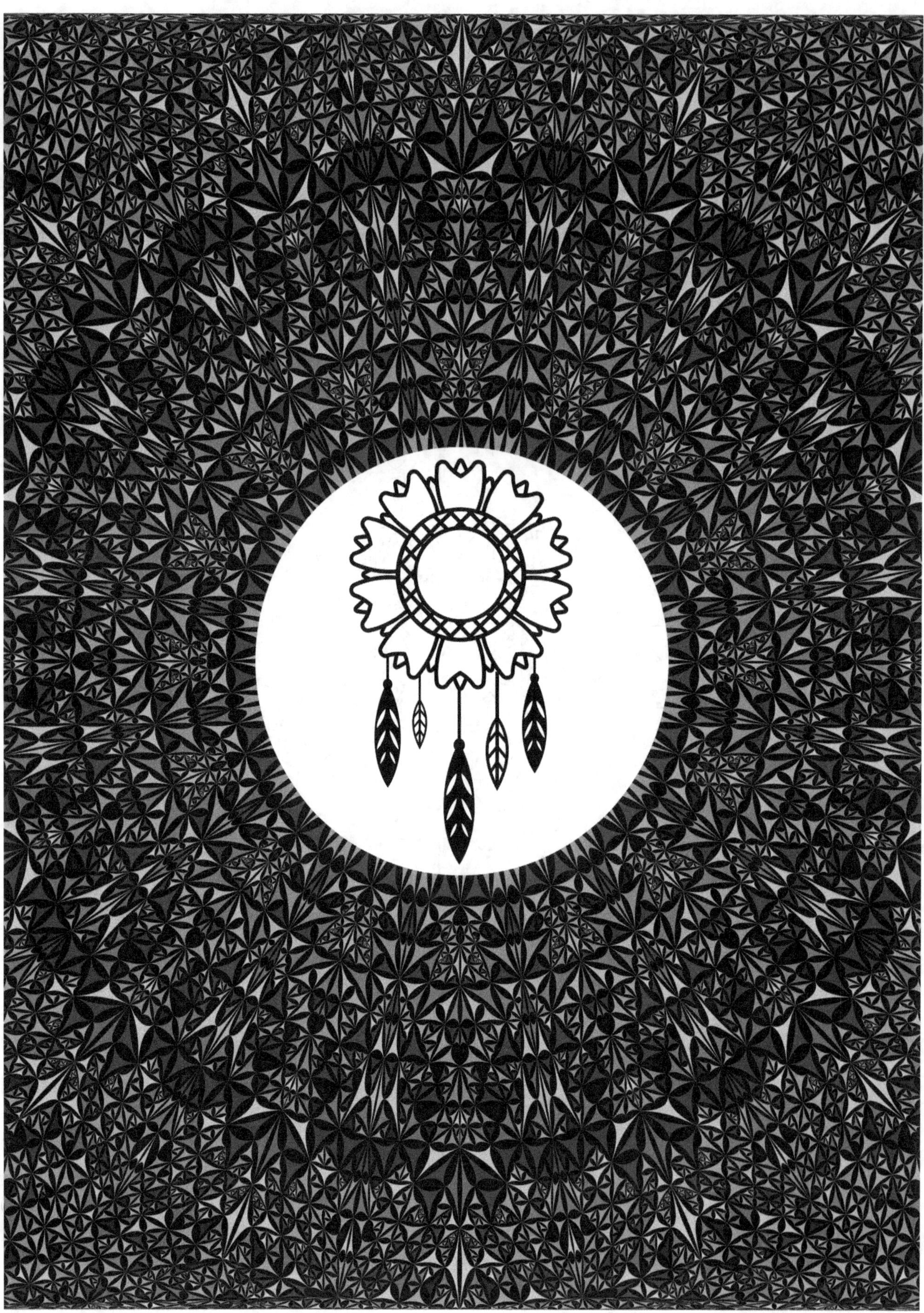

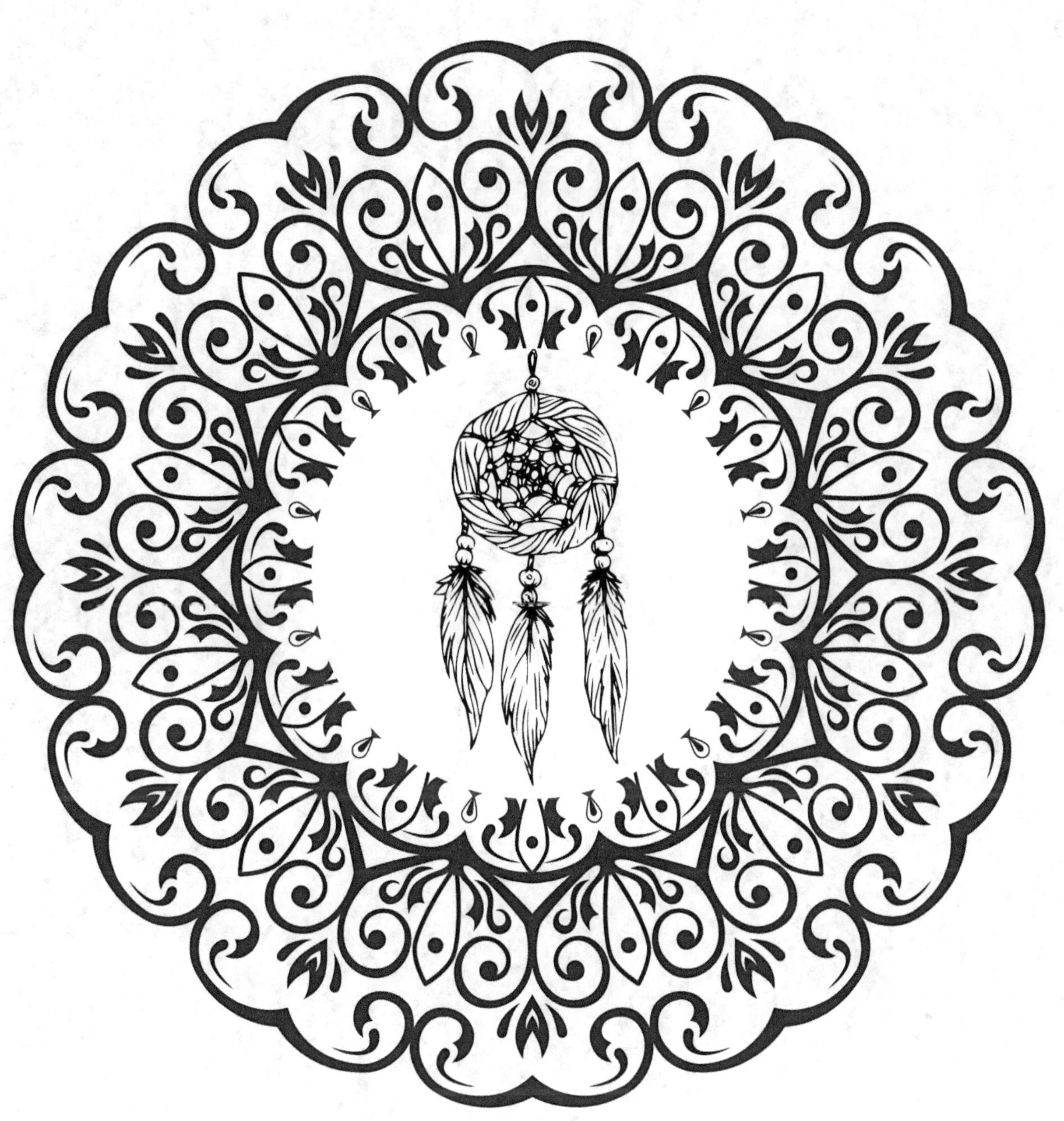

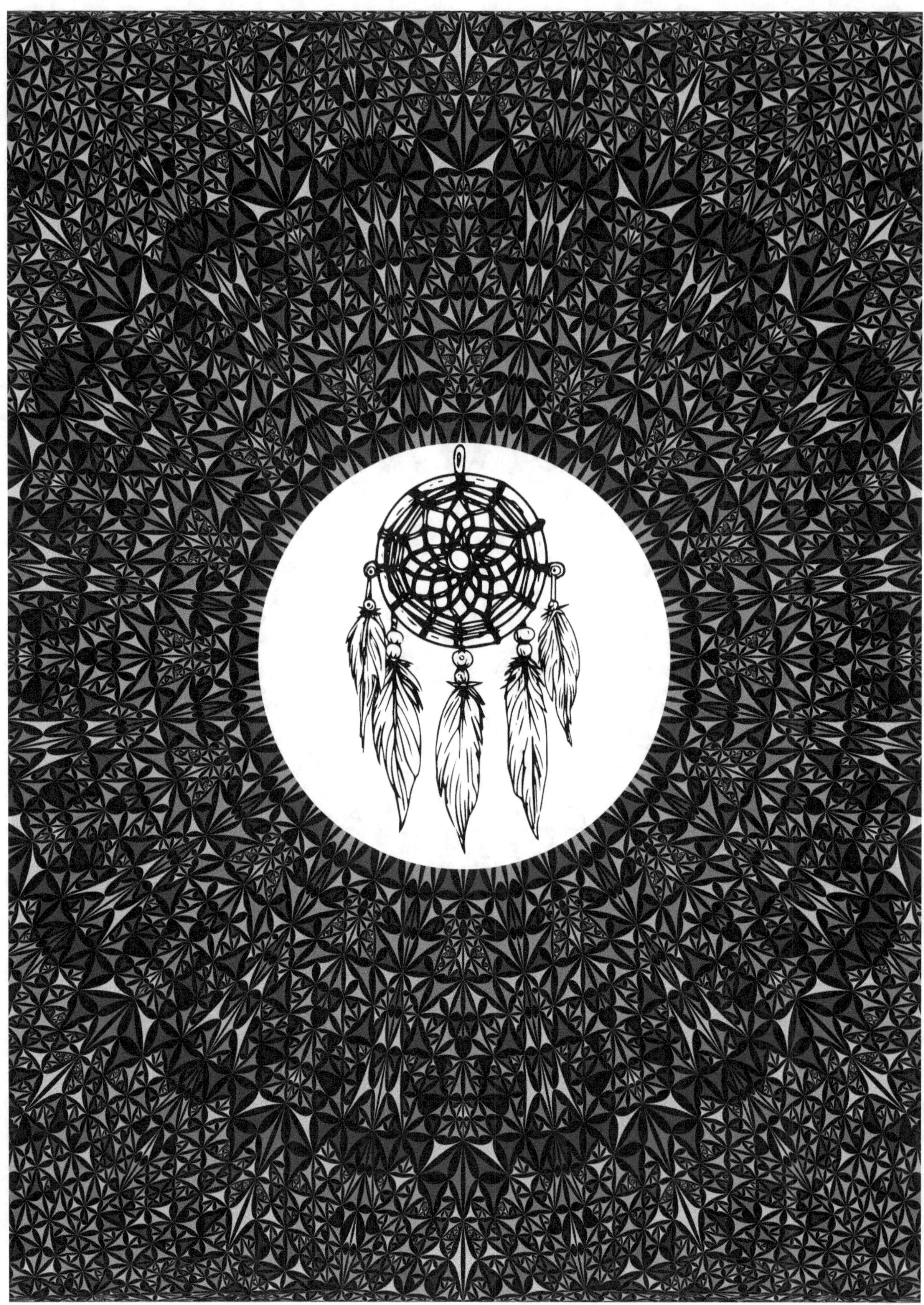

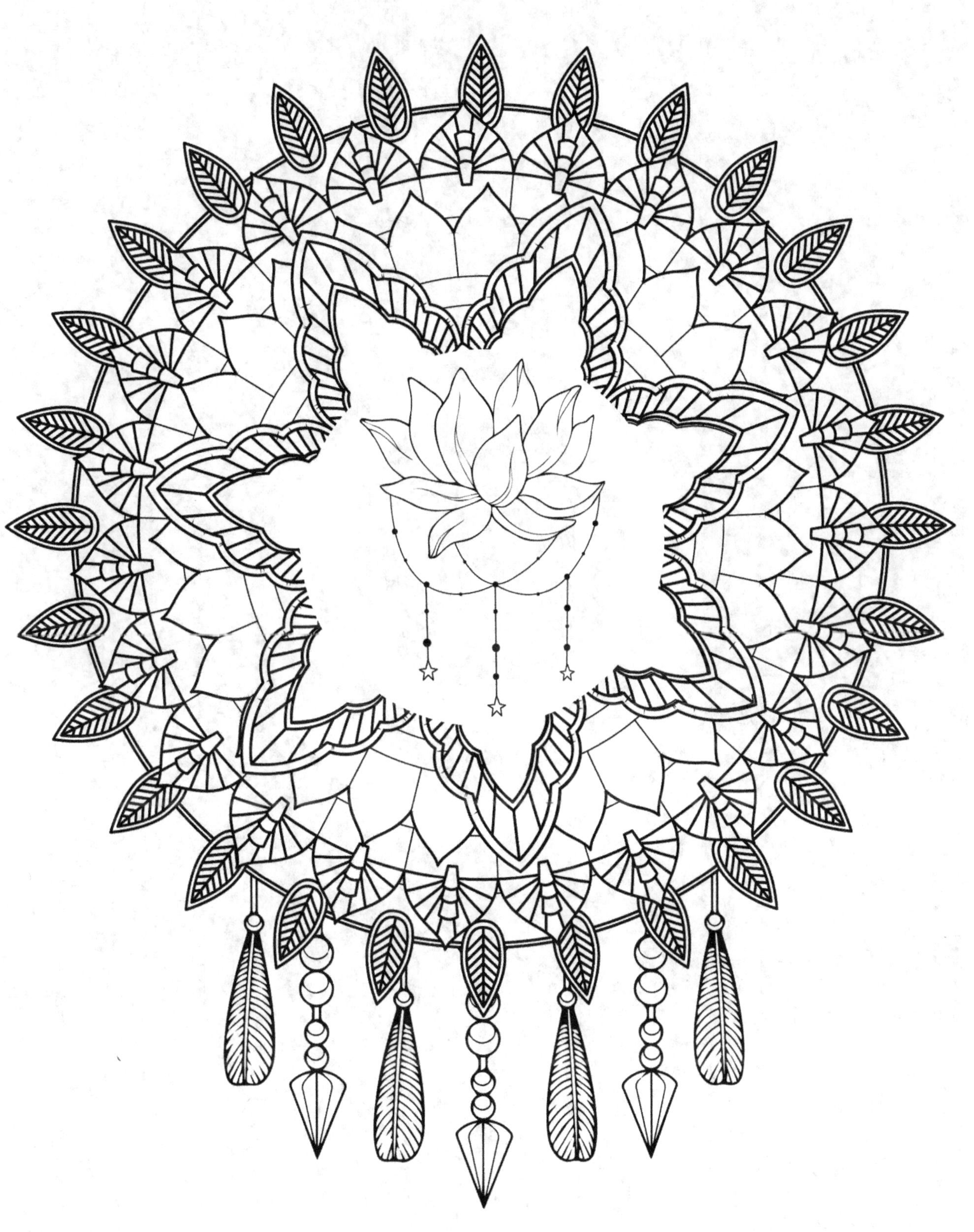

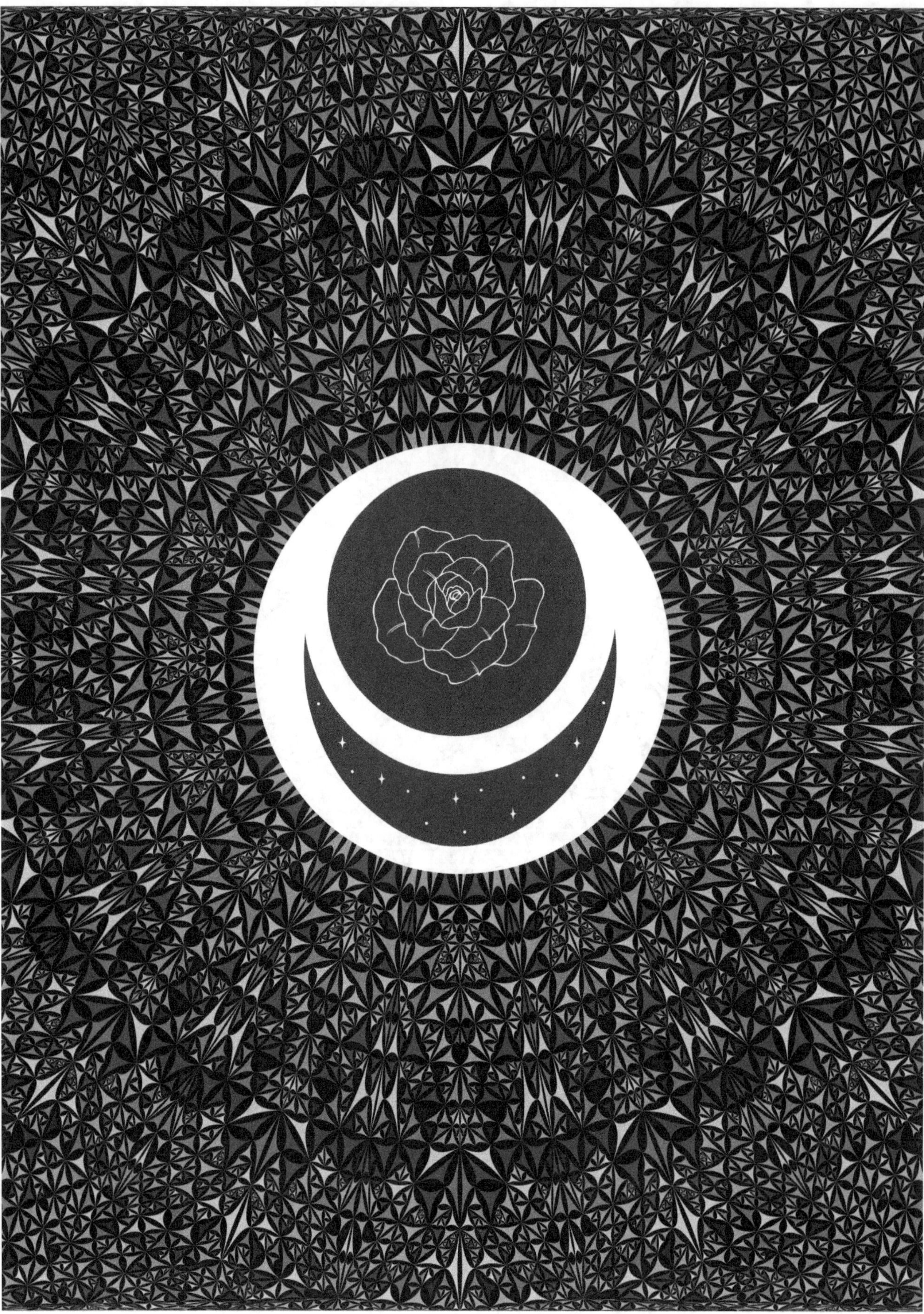

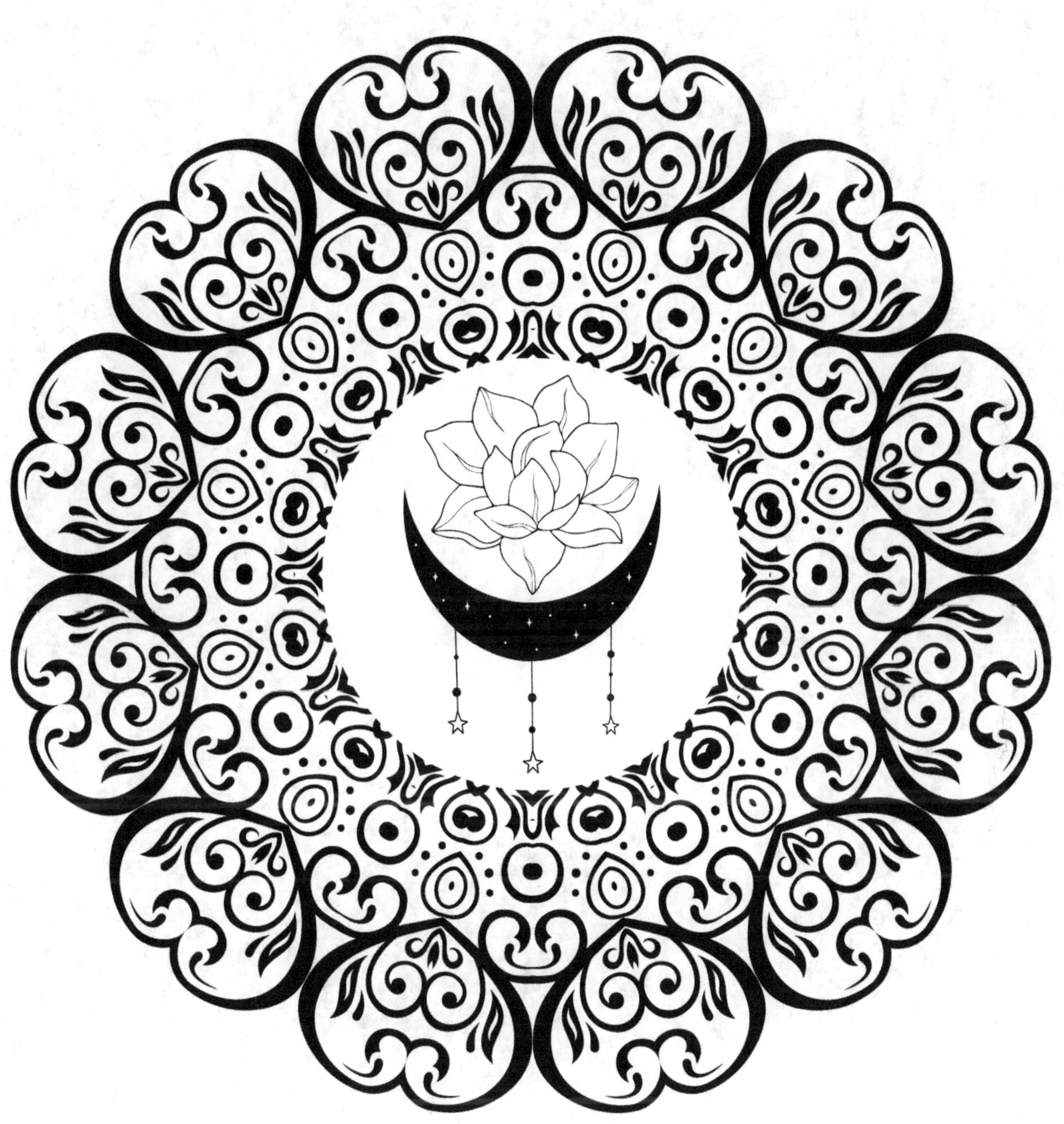

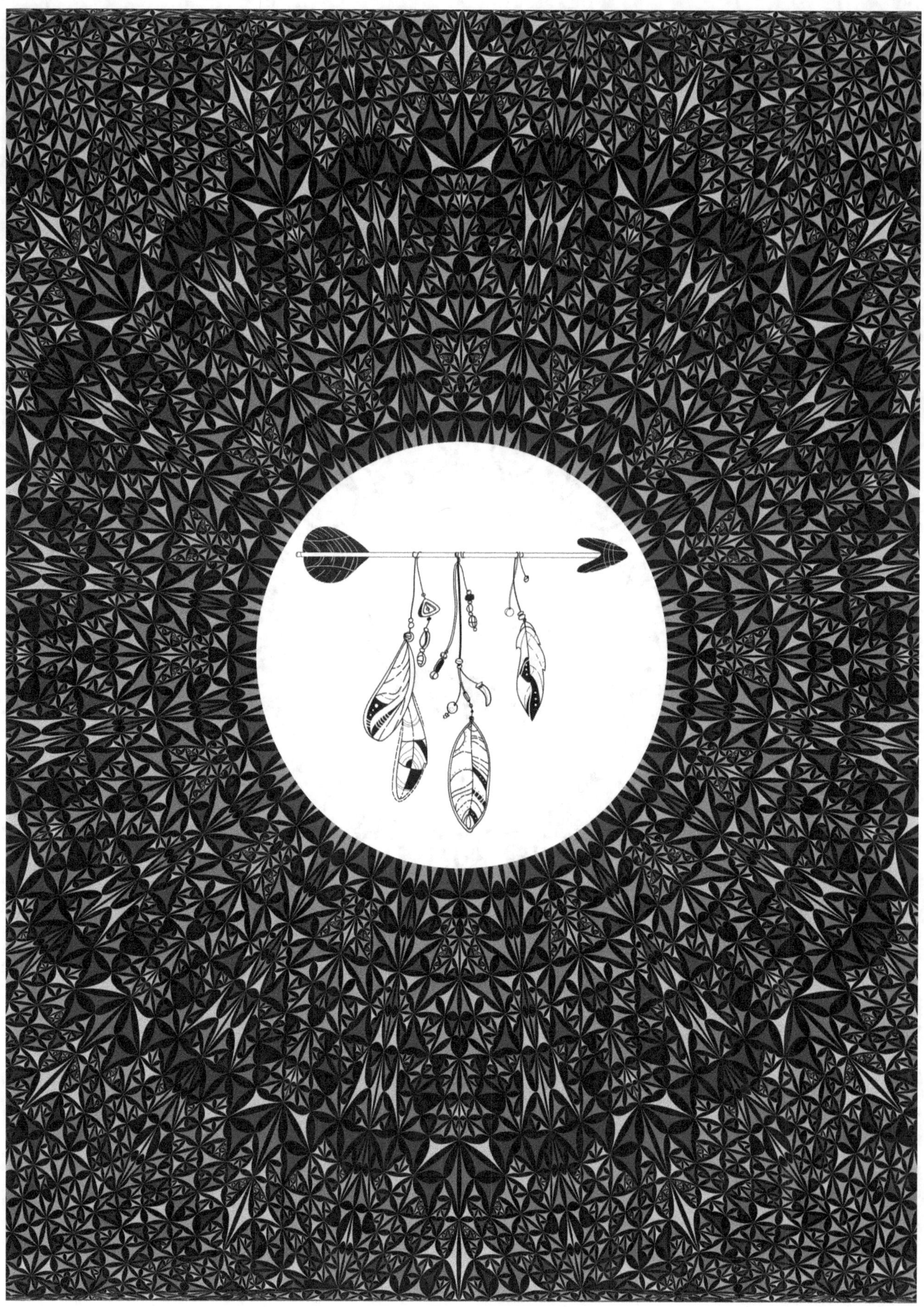

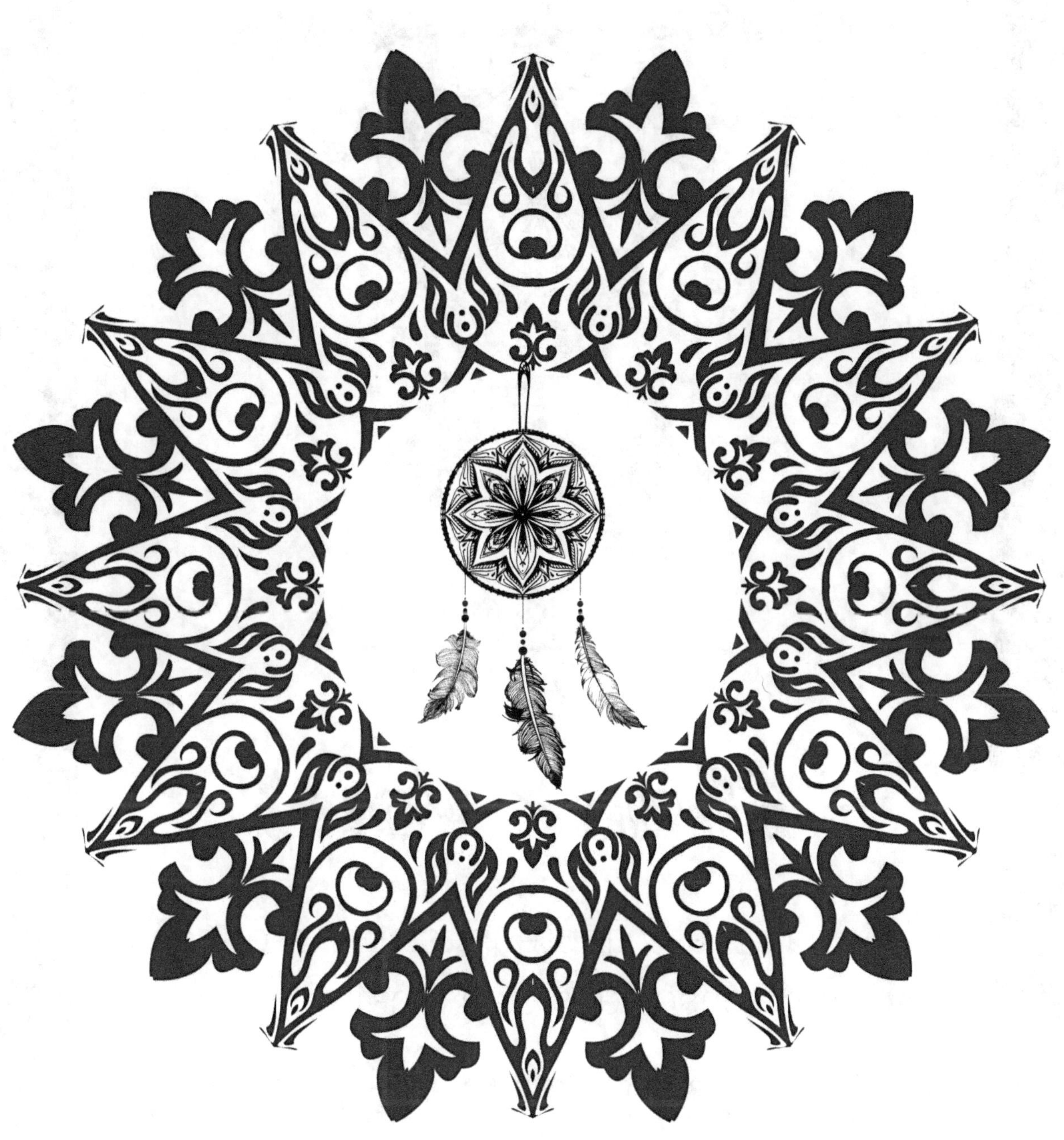

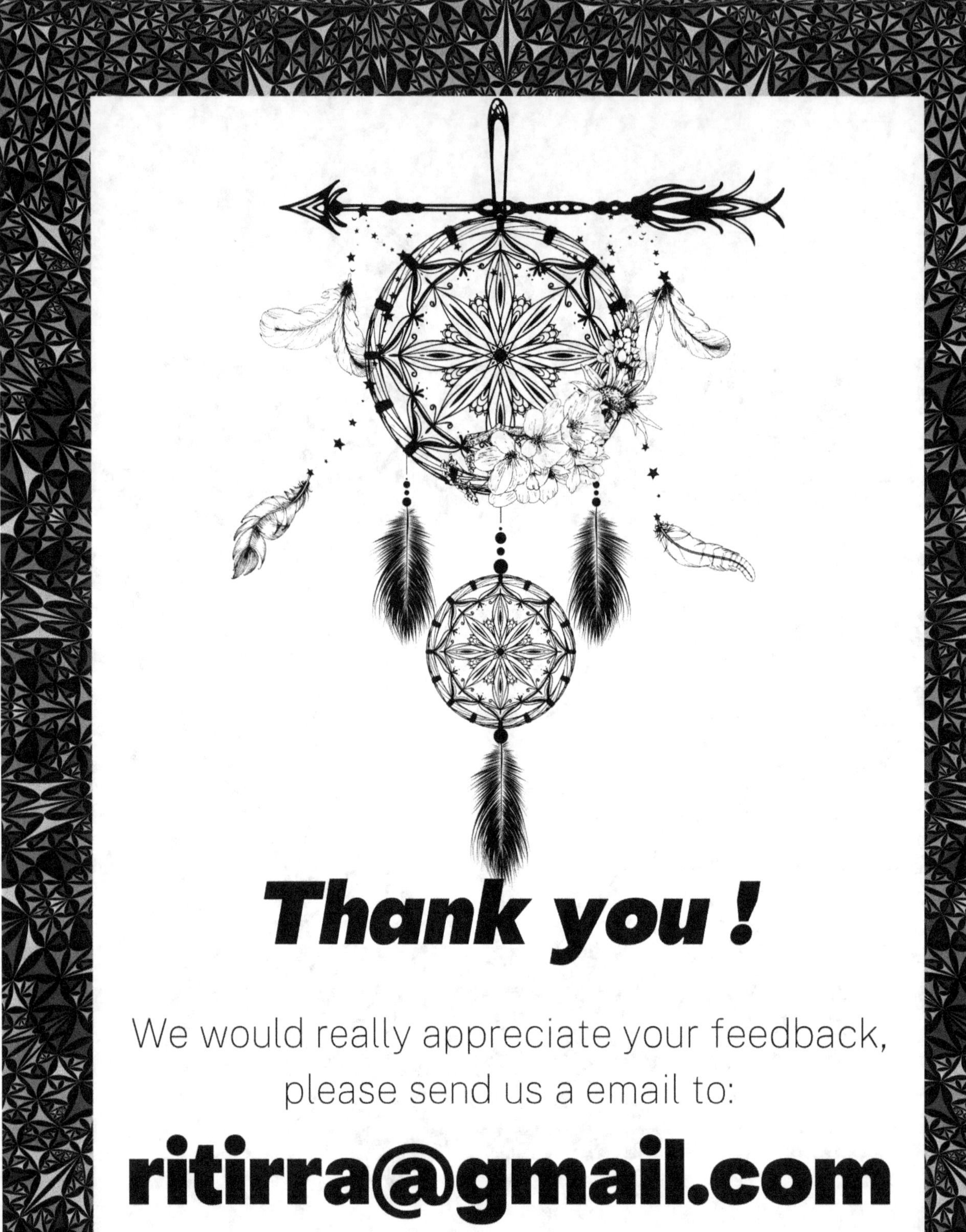

Thank you !

We would really appreciate your feedback,
please send us a email to:

ritirra@gmail.com